Louis Napoleon, E̶ ̶ ̶ ̶or of the French: A Biography

James Augustus

BIBLIOLIFE

LOUIS NAPOLEON,

EMPEROR OF THE FRENCH:

A Biography.

BY

JAMES AUGUSTUS ST. JOHN.

" Nothing extenuate, nor set down aught in malice "
SHAKESPEARE.

LONDON:

CHAPMAN AND HALL, 193, PICCADILLY.

1857.

TO

EDWARD HODGES BAILY, Esq., R.A.,

EQUALLY DISTINGUISHED FOR

HIS GENIUS AND HIS ADMIRABLE SOCIAL QUALITIES,

This Volume is Dedicated,

BY HIS SINCERE FRIEND,

THE AUTHOR.

PREFACE.

THIS is no party book. My aim in it has been to forestall, as far as possible, the decisions of posterity, and to paint Louis Napoleon as history will paint him, when it comes dispassionately to review his career. The moderation of my views may, perhaps, displease the extreme members of all parties. But I do not write for them. I address myself to that large body of Englishmen who love fair play in all things, and are able immediately to distinguish truth from its opposite.

In composing my narrative, I have consulted all the authorities accessible to me. From Frenchmen residing in England, and from Englishmen residing in France, I have obtained information calculated to throw light on particular points; communications have likewise been made to me by persons engaged in some of the transactions described, familiar with state affairs, and little disposed by their character to be hurried away by passion or dazzled by success. It has happened, too, that I have been placed in circumstances which have enabled me to form an opinion for myself. I was in France when the Revolution of July awakened the hopes of the whole Bonaparte family; I lived in Switzerland at the same time with Louis Napoleon; I visited Italy shortly after the failure of his expedition against the Pope; and I was again in Paris, mixing much in political society, during that eventful year which saw him raised to the Presidentship of the French Republic.

In spite of these advantages, I am fully sensible of the extreme difficulty of the subject. Republicans, Bourbonists, Bonapartists, Orleanists, impart the colour of their own passions to events, and consciously or unconsciously misrepresent whatever they relate. Against this natural tendency of party spirit I have had to guard as well as I could. Respect for myself would not permit me to become knowingly the instrument of any political faction, and respect for the public would restrain me from making any statement the grounds of which I had not carefully examined. Still I cannot flatter myself with the belief that I have fallen into no errors; but as my object has been to be at once frank and conscientious, I trust I shall — here in England at least — be frankly and conscientiously judged. Perhaps, even in France, I may be allowed by temperate and impartial politicians to have drawn a faithful picture of its present emperor, and to have described honestly and without prejudice the circumstances which have placed him where he is.

13 Grove End Road, St. John's Wood.
February 3rd, 1857.

CONTENTS.

CHAP. VI

HORTENSE AND THE EMPEROR ALEXANDER

CHAP. VII.

ESCAPE AND CONCEALMENT

CHAP. VIII.

EPISODE OF THE HUNDRED DAYS.

CHAP. IX.

GOING INTO EXILE.

CHAP. X.

INCIDENTS AT AIX.

CHAP XI.

ADVENTURES ON THE WAY TO CONSTANCE.

CHAP XII

ANECDOTES OF HIS BOYHOOD

CHAP. XIII.

THE COLLEGE OF AUGSBURG.

PART THE SECOND.

CHAPTER I.

THE BONAPARTES BEYOND THE ALPS.

CHAP. II.

LOUIS NAPOLEON ENGAGES IN THE INSURRECTION IN ROMAGNA.

CHAP. III.

HIS DISCOMFITURE AND FLIGHT.

CHAP. IV.

PERILOUS RETREAT FROM ANCONA.

CHAP. V.

LOUIS NAPOLEON VISITS AND PLOTS IN ENGLAND.

CHAP. VI.

SHIFTS THE SCENE OF ITS POLITICAL OPERATIONS TO
SWITZERLAND.

CHAP VII

HIS FIRST ATTEMPT AGAINST LOUIS PHILIPPE'S THRONE.

CHAP. VIII.

CROSSES THE ATLANTIC

CHAP. IX.

DEATH OF HORTENSE.—THE SWISS IN ARMS.

CHAP. X.

THE SCENE AGAIN CHANGES TO LONDON.

PART THE THIRD

CHAPTER I

THE CHÂTEAU OF HAM.

CHAP. II.

ESCAPE — ANECDOTES.

CHAP. VII.

THE COUP D'ÉTAT.

CHAP. VIII

THE MASSACRE OF DECEMBER

CHAP. IX.

THE PROGRESS. — THE EMPIRE.

CHAP. X.

THE RUSSIAN WAR.

CHAP. XI

ACTUAL POSITION OF LOUIS NAPOLEON.

LOUIS NAPOLEON,

EMPEROR OF THE FRENCH.

PART THE FIRST.

CHAPTER I.

DAWN OF IMPERIAL LIFE.

On the 20th of April, 1808, the roar of cannon announced to the people of Paris the birth of Louis Napoleon, son of Hortense, Queen of Holland. The power and glory of the French Empire had reached their culminating point; all Europe regarded with wonder and terror the fortunes of Napoleon; he created a number of regal satrapies, — Spain, Westphalia, Holland,—and bestowed them on his brothers; the generals, who had shared with him the dangers of the field of battle, he raised to the rank of princes; and to be connected with him by blood, by marriage, or by friendship, was to possess the unquestionable secret of success.

Hortense Fanny Beauharnais, daughter of the Empress Josephine, by a former marriage, was at this time living apart from her husband. Her union with Louis Bonaparte, founded neither in preference nor affection, had from the beginning been pre-eminently unhappy. The proud young beauty, despising the weakness, tameness, and superstitious terrors of her husband, bestowed all her admiration on the emperor, whose vast genius and energy for many years pervaded and impressed the whole public opinion of Christendom.

It was to answer some purpose not at present intelligible, that Napoleon and Josephine had effected this ill-assorted match. The husband and wife were not only indifferent to each other, but even before their marriage had shown a strong mutual repugnance which afterwards ripened into hatred, and converted their palace at the Hague into a scene of the most painful dissensions. Two hostile parties divided the court, and carried on a perpetual warfare of bickerings, intrigues, calumnies, outrages, and malevolence.

Louis, on arriving in Holland, determined as far as possible to conciliate the Dutch, but had unfortunately taken along with him a number of French courtiers, male and female, who, selecting the queen for their centre, revolved about her incessantly in a circle of vanity and frivolity, ridiculing the Dutch and their manners, and seeking to reproduce among the Dykes a second Paris. At length, under pretence of ill health, Hortense quitted the Hague, in search of better air, and proceeded to the château of St. Loo, situated at some distance from the capital; but very soon acquiring greater courage, effected her escape from Holland, and fled to be near the emperor in Paris.

The children of Hortense were at this time contemplated by Napoleon as the natural heirs of his grandeur. Her eldest son, about whose existence there hangs an extraordinary degree of mystery, died on the 5th of May, 1807, at what age writers are not agreed.* It was on the occasion of this

* De Bausset, possibly through inadvertence, says the child died at the age of seven. But Hortense had at the time been married only five years and a few months. Her union with Louis Bonaparte took place, according to some writers, Jan. 2nd, 1802, according to others, on the 4th, or 5th, or 7th. Felix Wouters, who had carefully studied the affairs of Napoleon's family, is unable to fix the day of this unlucky marriage. When he speaks of the wife (Les Bonapartes, 271), he says she was married Jan. 2nd; when he speaks of the husband, he says he was married Jan. 4th (p. 351).

bereavement, that the idea of a divorce from Josephine presented itself to Napoleon's mind. He
at first imparted his views to a few friends, cautiously, rather alluding to the design as a thing
which might be, than as to a fixed and organised
plan ; though it can hardly be doubted that he
had already in secret determined upon the course he
should pursue. The divorce took place, the marriage with Marie Louise was brought about by
policy, and in the spring of 1811 the King of Rome
was born, to annihilate, as was then supposed, the
hopes and prospects of the sons of Hortense.

The Bonaparte family, though united by interest
and by affection, liable however to much fluctuation
and caprice, was from time to time torn by discord, by
jealousy, by inordinate ambition. Most of Napoleon's
brothers adhered to him, and submitted to the despotism of his temper. But Lucien, presuming to have
a will of his own, was for this cut off, together with
all his children, from the chance of succeeding to the
imperial dignity. In case of accident therefore to the
King of Rome, the sons of Hortense, Napoleon and
Louis, were still regarded as the true heirs to the
throne, which had been established with so much
bloodshed, perfidy, ambition, energy, and genius.

How soon the circumstances by which men are

surrounded begin to act upon their minds, and co-operate in forming their characters, philosophers have not yet been able to decide. It is probable that, from the moment of birth, everything which befalls an individual should be reckoned among the causes that combine to fashion his idiosyncracies, and render him what he afterwards becomes. It is a trite observation that men depend very much for their qualities, both moral and intellectual, on their mothers, who not only impart to them their physical temperament, but influence, in their original springs, their passions and principles.

Hortense was a woman in all respects remarkable, — beautiful in person, in organisation peculiarly delicate, feeble in health, flexible in principles; she yet, when a persuasion had once been adopted, displayed so much tenacity of purpose as to expose her all her life to the charge of obstinacy. In courage, whether active or passive, she was indomitable. To the unfortunate, she was kind and generous, strongly affectionate in her friendships, and towards her children, tender, gentle, and full of solicitude. But her ruling passion was attachment to Napoleon, which, in times of great difficulty and danger, overmastered even her maternal feelings, and led her for his sake to set the whole world at defiance.

To comprehend the effect produced on the mind of Louis Napoleon by the instruction and discipline of such a mother, it will be necessary to follow his career almost from the cradle ; and if I appear too lavish of anecdotes and minute details, my apology must be the desire by which I am actuated to explain the character and account for the fortunes of the man, to whom the French people have sacrificed so much.

Vicissitude is confessedly the law of human life. Everybody experiences it more or less; but in the whole history of modern times, there are few examples of individuals who have passed through greater or more numerous changes than Louis Napoleon. Born in a palace, and for a while the heir presumptive of the greatest monarch in Europe, he was afterwards thrown headlong from that high estate, and condemned in obscurity and exile to associate with the sons of humble tradesmen and farmers ; to be to-day the companion of cardinals, popes, and kings, and to sleep to-morrow on a heap of stones in the street, in the disguise of a livery servant ; to lie hidden during eight days in a burning fever, in the midst of Austrian troops, who were eager to take his life ; to fight as a common soldier and a rebel, in the hope of overthrowing a hateful form of despotism ; to have his

brother die in his arms; to wander about in sickness,
hunger, and dejection; to take refuge in common
taverns; to owe his life to an English passport; to
tread the soil of France as an outlaw at the peril of
his life; to organise repeated insurrections, to be in
prison, to lie in a dungeon; to write treatises on
Pauperism and the Sugar Question; to mingle with
the haughty nobles of England at a tournament, to
be the President of a Republic, to take advantage of
the opportunity thus afforded him to make himself
Emperor; to be the ally on terms of equality of the
strongest government in Europe; and, in conjunction
with Great Britain, to subdue the armies of Russia,
and compel her Czar to sue humbly for peace in that
capital which, forty-two years before, on the self-same
day, he had entered as a conqueror.

Such is the career of the man whose fortunes
I have to describe in this narrative. I shall perform
my task as far as possible with impartiality, praising
what is praiseworthy, censuring freely what is wrong,
and endeavouring in all cases to draw, from the example under consideration, lessons advantageous to
mankind.

When two years and a half old, that is, on the
fourth of November, 1810, Louis Napoleon was bap-
tized at Fontainebleau by his uncle, Cardinal Fesch,

Napoleon and Marie Louise being his godfather and
godmother. Hortense did not, as some writers appear
to suppose, reside in the Tuileries, but in her own
palace, whence she almost daily went to dine with the
Emperor. Like most other great men, Napoleon was
extremely exact in the observance of time, and used
to scold the members of his family if they were not
punctually at the Tuileries as the clock struck six.
Frequently, therefore, Hortense was able to devote but
very few minutes to dressing. Her valet de chambre
on these occasions was put greatly out of humour by
her haste and impatience. " Never mind," she used to
say, " how my hair is done, only be quick, that I may
be at the Tuileries in time." " But your Majesty,"
the man would reply deprecatingly, " will absolutely
ruin me in the opinion of the Emperor. What will
he say if he sees your hair huddled up after this
fashion ? " " Don't be alarmed," she replied, " there
are plenty of ladies about the court, on whose heads
you can exhibit your skill. The only point I insist
on is quickness."

Hortense possessed the most beautiful and luxuriant hair, of a light shining blonde, tinged with an
ashen hue, which imparted to it an extraordinary appearance. It was long enough to reach the ground,
and when she sat upon a chair to have it dressed, she

suffered it to fall over her whole figure like a veil, and
trail on all sides upon the floor. Even at such times
her two little sons were always with her, and used
often to amuse themselves by hiding in turn under
their mother's hair, and bolting out suddenly to produce a laugh. When she was dressed they generally
went down with her to the carriage-door, one of the
little fellows carrying her gloves and shawl, while the
other performed the office of a page, and bore her
train. Napoleon did not keep late hours, so that in
most cases she returned to her children about nine
o'clock.

CHAP. II.

THE MOTHER'S DISCIPLINE.

THE physical constitution of Hortense was peculiar, and no doubt affected to some extent that of her sons. She was liable to the most excruciating head-aches, during which her body became so cold that the hottest baths often failed to restore warmth to it, till nature recovered its empire. This peculiarity of temperament made her always desirous of possessing a bedroom with a southern aspect, and she used to bewail herself with extraordinary pathos whenever circumstances compelled her to sleep in a room look-ing towards the north.

At that time she possessed all the luxuries and en-joyments which money or power could command. At St. Leu, five leagues from Paris, she had a charming country residence, where the Empress Josephine often came to visit her. Here the children passed their time in the midst of delightful gardens, abounding with the rarest and sweetest flowers, and enjoyed a healthy and bracing atmosphere. The queen occa-

sionally drove out in what the French call a char-à-
banc, resembling in construction the Irish jaunting
car, with a partition down the middle, in which
people sit back to back. In this she went constantly
with her children through the woods of Mont
Morency, and visited all the picturesque points in the
neighbourhood

In the evening, the persons who happened to be
visiting at St. Leu assembled in the drawing-room,
and, to pass away the time, had recourse to all sorts
of harmless amusements. Now and then the children
were suffered to be present; but when the hour of
bedtime arrived, no prayers nor entreaties on their
part could induce her to allow them to remain a
moment longer. An anecdote is related, which at
once shows how rigidly she adhered to her system of
discipline, and the effects it produced on the dispositions of her sons. One evening Louis the younger
had been sent to bed, while Napoleon had been
allowed to remain up a little later. In conjunction
with her female attendants, he had projected for his
mamma some little agreeable surprise, and wished to
remain up to observe the effect of it. The ladies,
however, had told him that it was to be a secret,
which caused the poor boy great perplexity. When
at length Hortense thought he had staid up long

enough, she wished him good night, and bade him go to bed at once. He entreated and cried, but to no purpose ; his mother's will was a will of iron, and he went. But when afterwards she learned the child's motive for desiring to sit up, she was so grieved, that it entirely spoiled the pleasure which had been prepared for her. Still she had the satisfaction to discover that her gallant little boy would rather suffer punishment than betray a secret.

It is of course no distinction, to say that Hortense was extremely fond of her children ; — because in this she only resembled most other mothers; but her care, tenderness, and solicitude, went beyond what is common in situations so elevated as that which she then occupied. Her maternal fondness exposed her at times to unnecessary suffering and alarm. On one occasion, she had permitted a young lady at the Château to take out the children for a drive through the woods. A large party of gay and fashionable persons from Paris had already assembled in the salon ; night was setting in, and numbers of those, who then professed themselves her admirers, entreated her to sing some of her own beautiful ballads. Her courtesy and good nature induced her to comply, but every one present could perceive that an unusual gloom, not unmixed with terror, had settled

upon the mind of the queen. At length she heard
a slight noise overhead, which made her stop in the
midst of her singing. First a paleness, then a flush
came over her. It was the sound of little feet running
to and fro in the nursery. She turned to one of the
ladies in waiting, and exclaimed, "What, are they
come back, then?"

"Did not your Majesty know," replied the lady,
" that they have been at home an hour or more?"

"If I had," observed Hortense, "I should have
been spared an hour of no ordinary anxiety."

As Hortense's health was far from good, she sometimes found it necessary to undertake, for its improvement, little journeys into different parts of France;
and on these occasions, it was not always thought
advisable to take her sons along with her. They
were then left under the care of her mother, the
Empress Josephine, whose tender and susceptible
nature peculiarly qualified her to watch over children.
M. de Marmold, steward of the queen's household,
remained with the boys, as well as the Abbé Bertrand, who had the care of their education. When
Hortense returned from Aix in Savoy, she remained
a few days at St. Leu, and then set out for the sea
shore, taking her sons along with her. She was now
accompanied by a more numerous suite, and took up

her residence at a château near the beach, in the
vicinity of Dieppe, for the benefit of sea bathing and
sea air.   Louis Napoleon appeared at first to have
inherited the delicate health and feeble frame of his
mother; and if he has since given proofs of great
firmness and vigour of body, it is probable that he
owes the happiness of possessing these qualities to his
having been thrown, in early life, into positions of
difficulty and danger.

An anecdote is related of his childhood, which
shows at once how easily he was terrified, and how
quickly he could shake off his fears.   At four years
old, when he first saw a chimney-sweep, he was
greatly alarmed, and threw himself into the arms of
his governess.   The theories of Jean Jacques were
just then popular in France, among all who undertook the education of children.   Madame de Boubers,
who watched over the early development of Louis
Napoleon's faculties, seized upon this occasion to in-
culcate a lesson of humanity and self-command.
Knowing that the apprehensions of children should
not be violently repressed, she took him on her knee,
soothed him with caresses, and dissipated for ever
his fear of those little black men, who may almost be
said to live in the chimneys of Paris.   The future
emperor's governess appears to have been a woman

of gentle sympathies. She pitied those wandering Savoyards, who, far from their homes, earned a scanty subsistence, by pursuing one of the meanest and most dangerous employments to which the exigencies of a great city give rise. The pity which she herself felt, she sought to inspire into the mind of her pupil, and her sentiments, delivered in nurses' dialect, appear to have interested the child's feelings.

A few months later, being asleep one morning with his brother, the nurse left the room for a moment. During her absence, a young Savoyard, as black as Erebus, descended the chimney, and coming out into the nursery, shook himself, and filled the whole chamber with a dark cloud. Louis Napoleon, a light sleeper, awoke, and was again seized with terror on beholding a sweep. But soon calling to mind what Madame de Boubers had told him about the poverty and misery of the little Savoyards, he climbed over the railings of his cot, and running across the room in his night-shirt, and mounting on a chair, took forth from a drawer his pocket money, and gave it, purse and all, to the little sweep. He then tried to climb back into his bed, but found it impracticable, upon which his brother called the nurse.

He had hitherto been accustomed, when he went out for a walk, to carry about his pocket money with

him; and his mother had taught him to regard it
as a privilege to be allowed to give it away. But
having now, however, disposed of his whole stock at
once, his teachers, like genuine disciples of Rousseau,
turned the incident into an occasion for a little moral
lecturing. Had this happened to any common boy,
it would hardly have interested any one beyond his
mother, or at most the family circle; but the court
adulators, converting the incident into an historical
event, had the scene painted on a porcelain vase,
which they presented to Hortense on her birth-day.
Having more money than she knew how to spend
judiciously, Josephine thought this an excellent opportunity for indulging in a little domestic extravagance, and formed the design of reproducing the
sketch on the vase in a grand oil painting. Possibly,
however, the public disasters of France, which came
soon after to occupy the minds of the Bonaparte
family, prevented the execution of this project. At
any rate, I have never seen such a picture referred to
in the history of French art.

CHAP. III.

TERROR AND FLIGHT.

UP to a certain age, the history of a child is involved in the history of its parents, which must therefore to some extent be related in order to convey a just idea of the child itself.

Louis Napoleon had scarcely attained the age of six years, when the fortunes of the French empire were over-cast by those terrible reverses, which impressed a new character on the whole of Europe. I have already observed that from the period of his divorce from Josephine, Napoleon's star, to use his own jargon, began to pale. It may, or may not, have been affected by that circumstance. He probably felt, that by allying himself with the house of Hapsburg, he had passed out of the category of a revolutionary chief, irresistible, through the attachment of the people, into that of a quasi-legitimate sovereign, upheld partly by ancient prejudices, partly by military force.

The strength of Napoleon's character, together

c

with the resources of his mind, had been extravagantly exaggerated by the various populations of Europe, which found it impracticable to detach his figure from the vast *ensemble* created by the revolution, and contemplate it apart. His genius was military, mathematical, coordinating. He looked upon the whole world as a camp, in which everything was to be subjected rigidly to discipline, in exact conformity with a system invented and administered by himself. He viewed with extreme jealousy, or perhaps I should rather say with extreme dislike, the slightest symptoms of a creative mind in others, and hence the inveteracy of his hostility to literature and every form of independent thought. He hated, he persecuted, he crushed everything which had a tendency to excite the love of liberty. What he desired was obedience, servile, absolute, and during a long series of years he found it in the French people.

Up to a certain point his conduct was regulated by new ideas, and so far he was victorious; but being unable to lay aside altogether the traditional policy of the old worn out monarchies of the continent, he attempted to amalgamate the moth-eaten with the new, and became the victim of this experiment.

Having resolved on the conquest of Russia, and therefore considering it already his own, he refused to reconstruct the kingdom of Poland, which would, he fancied, have been to diminish the value of his prize, and by this act of selfishness ensured and deserved the total overthrow that succeeded.

But it is not my design to dwell at any length on events so well known. After the Battle of Leipsic, Napoleon retreated, and the shattered fragments of his army were hopelessly dispersed. Historians, reviewing calmly from a distance the events of those times, have attempted to show how Napoleon might have concentrated his forces, recalled his generals from Spain, Italy, and the low countries, and baffled all his enemies, even at the eleventh hour.

But the French people have no sympathy with a falling dynasty, and it was his familiarity with this characteristic of theirs which rendered Napoleon so solicitous to prevent all knowledge of his disasters from spreading, especially in the capital. Spies and informers had always formed a part of the government of France, and he had converted their calling into an institution of his empire. Anticipating universal defection, he determined by restraint, punishment, and terror, to coerce the babbling propensities of his subjects. He had taught them by experience the spirit of his government. The slightest symptom of disaffection had been suppressed by imprisonment, by dungeons, by death; and now that he was beginning to stand, like the lion at bay, in the midst of relentless enemies, it was not probable that he would be slower to strike, or that his vengeance would be less terrible.

It was only in faint whispers, therefore, and by slow degrees, that the approach of the allied armies was revealed. Everybody felt that the least allusion to a defeat of the Emperor would be regarded as high treason. Yet the whole body of his partisans, his dependents, his family, were profoundly interested in obtaining some insight into what was taking place beyond the walls of the capital. From them consequently it could not be long concealed that all Europe had risen against the tyrant, and that a prodigious army, animated by the fiercest passions, was already on the French soil. Napoleon in his day of power had displayed little moderation or mercy, and he and his now expected none from those whom he had driven into exile, or goaded by his oppression.

As the allied army advanced, the rural inhabitants of France fled before it. Nothing was anticipated but the most fearful retaliation, the burning of towns and villages, slaughter, outrage, pillage. Under this impression, scenes of distress and misery were everywhere produced by the people's own fears. All those who could hope from their proximity to reach Paris, rushed in headlong flight towards it.

The roads were thronged as far as the eye could reach with the humbler classes of all ages, some driving before them the little furniture they possessed, piled upon carts and waggons; they who had no vehicles bore what they considered most valuable on their heads or shoulders, while the women carried their babies in their arms, and led their young children by the hand.

Of the aged, they who were able to walk accompanied their families; but the majority, too feeble to keep pace with their more robust relatives, were either abandoned in their half empty dwellings, or dropped, and perished by the way. The French peasants, ignorant of the manners and character of their neighbours, pictured to themselves the allies as fierce, unrelenting savages, or even cannibals, and were terrified by the creations of their own fancies.

While this vast multitude was rolling like a tumultuous ocean towards the capital, in the hope of finding protection there, thousands of opulent families were leaving it hastily in their carriages on the opposite side, imagining they would be more safe, far away in the châteaux of the central and southern provinces.

The government had not as yet been completely paralysed. The defence of Paris, and the safety of Marie Louise with her son, the young King of Rome, had been entrusted to Joseph Bonaparte, more remarkable for social and civil qualities than for generalship or ambition. Feeling, however, the responsibility of his situation, he called together the supreme council, at which his brother Jerome was present, together with Marie Louise herself. This young woman, not then twenty years of age, listened in silence while Joseph read aloud that letter of Napoleon, in which he says, "I would rather my son were at the bottom of the Seine than in the hands of the allies." In obedience to the imperative orders of Napoleon, preparations were made for the defence of the city,—the Empress and her son were presented to the national guard, who solemly and with enthusiasm undertook their defence. A strong force under Marshals Mortier and Marmont was pushed forward in advance of the walls, and it was hoped that the place might hold out till Napoleon could come up with an army for its relief.

The fears of the Parisians, which were now in a state of extraordinary activity gave rise to several incidents of an extremely ludicrous character. The old French houses abound with small closets, and in these the rich now huddled together their most valuable effects, jewels, plate, porcelain, costly dresses. In some cases the anxious proprietors, bewildered by terror, added to their other treasures magnificent time pieces, which, having been wound up for eight days, went on ticking and striking, and thus betrayed to the neighbours their place of concealment.

Hortense and her attendants shared all the fears and agonies of the French people, and passed the hours which intervened between the news of Napoleon's defeat, and her flight from Paris in a state of indescribable alarm. Louis, ex-king of Holland, was at this time living in Paris, at the house of his mother, but no personal intercourse had for a long while taken place between the husband and wife. He was in fact a person of extreme insignificance, whom no one invited to take part in public deliberations, or ever thought of consulting on any subject. Into the grounds of his separation from Hortense, I have not thought fit to inquire. If they did not live together, and seldom or never met, they sometimes corresponded on subjects connected with their

children, for whose well being Louis, at wide intervals, affected considerable solicitude.

During the night of terror and anxiety which pre-
ceded Hortense's flight from the capital, Louis attempted, in his imbecile way, to exercise his authority
as a husband.   Almost everybody in Paris, at the in-
stigation of fear or self-interest, was labouring to
impart to his or her countenance a legitimate expression with which to receive the Bourbons.   It was
now generally discovered that Napoleon ought to be
detested as a tyrant, that there was chivalry, poetry,
with thrilling and superb souvenirs in the worship
of the ancient dynasty, and upon nearly all lips im-
precations fluttered against the falling empire.   It
was not in Hortense's nature, even had she not
stood within the proscribed circle, to participate in
baseness like this.   If she clung to her friends in
the palmy hour of their fortune, she clung to them
still more closely in adversity; and therefore, whatever other faults may be laid to her charge, she
never could be accused, like so many of Napoleon's
friends, connections, and adherents, of bowing her
knee to the rising sun.

After having undergone extraordinary trouble and
excitement, sheer weariness at length overcame her,
and she sank into a profound sleep.   The lady who

had served her in the capacity of a reader, and now watched over her with much kindness, was soon constrained by a messenger from the ex-king to rouse her unfortunate mistress. There is no little confusion in the accounts transmitted to us of this night's proceedings. Louis's letters, the contents of which had been represented to the queen's attendants as of the highest importance, merely stated that the empress Marie Louise, not considering herself in safety, was about to quit Paris with her son. Hortense replied to her husband that she knew all this before, and having dismissed her women, endeavoured to sleep again.

Scarcely were her eyelids closed, however, when a second messenger arrived, bringing the intelligence that the empress, surrounded by her terror-stricken suite, had abandoned the capital, and that it consequently would not be safe for her to remain any longer in it with her children. What answer she vouchsafed her husband on this occasion is not stated, but being devoured by the desire of sleep, she once more lay down to snatch, if possible, a few moments of delicious oblivion. But Louis's marital solicitude was indefatigable; and again a third time he wrote to say, that she must decidedly leave Paris after the empress. It is probable that this time her answer

savoured less of submission and obedience than
Louis thought becoming; for upon the receipt of it,
he immediately sent to demand that the children
should be given up to him.

There are moments in all our lives when we
appear to lay aside the principles by which we are
habitually guided, and act like our own moral
antipodes. This mother, so tender, so watchful, so
absolutely bound up in her children, now without
the least struggle or remonstrance, relinquished them
to her weak and wayward husband, who, however,
had no sooner gained his point, than not knowing
what he should do with such a charge, he sent them
back again, observing, very judiciously, that they
were too young to be separated from their mother.
In this way the whole night was passed; and when
the morning came, the poor queen, though her
courage still held out, felt altogether exhausted with
sleeplessness and fatigue.

The women of her suite now crowded about her
with tears and lamentations, some grieving that they
must part from their friends, others that they must
part from her. One poor lady had been confined
during the night, and therefore could not choose but
remain behind. Throughout her whole life, Hortense
possessed the secret of attaching people to her, and

in spite of the fickleness of the French character,
I make no doubt that her friends and dependents
experienced much sorrow at the prospect of a separation, which, for aught they could then see, might
prove eternal.

All Paris was in an uproar. Everybody seemed
to be running to and fro ; here a string of carriages
shot along rapidly, there a body of national guards
hurried towards the walls, swearing vehemently
that they would defend them to the last drop of
their blood ; generals were sitting in council, aide-de-
camps, and other officers were bearing messages or
bringing intelligence, and the wives of those soldiers
who were absent with Napoleon clamourously be-
sieged the palace of the queen.

Everybody blamed Marie Louise for disappearing
with the young king of Rome, whose presence might
have inspired the national guards with courage to
defend the capital. Hortense promised to continue
in Paris with her children, and the declaration of
her resolve was received by the soldiers with loud
shouts and acclamations. Even at the age of six years,
therefore Louis Napoleon began to influence the
destinies of France. Presently, however, the news
spread like wildfire that the Cossacks had been
seen on the plains of Vertus, and it was felt that

they were only the vanguard of the allied army.
The military authorities, having examined the defences of Paris, declared the place to be untenable.
Hortense was accordingly absolved from her engagement, and vehemently urged by all the friends of
the Bonaparte family to escape, if possible, with her
children.

She in consequence determined to quit Paris that
night, and remain till morning at Versailles.   But
ere she set out, Madame Doumerc, who had always
expressed a strong attachment for her, came to say
that her mother possessed a country house at Glatigny,
where she entreated the queen to put up, rather
than at an inn.   This kind offer was accepted, and
about nine o'clock at night the little cortege set out.
Hortense herself, with the two boys Napoleon and
Louis, occupied one carriage, governesses and nurses
filled the second, the queen's female reader and her
femme-de-chambre had along with them the royal
jewels in a third carriage, and a fourth containing
the women servants brought up the rear.   As the
Cossacks were out scouring the country in all
directions, a courier was sent ahead, with orders if he
discovered the enemy to fire off a pistol, upon which
the carriages were to return to Paris.

CHAP IV.

THE QUEEN IN DANGER WITH HER CHILDREN.

THEY reached Glatigny, however, without interruption, though at a late hour in the night. The
queen saw her children put to bed, and then retired
herself, as well as her attendants, to snatch if possible a little sleep. Overcome by fatigue, they did
sleep, but were very soon awakened by the roar
of the cannon with which the allies were battering
the feeble defences of Paris. It was felt at once
there was no further safety at Glatigny, and rousing
the children, they dressed themselves speedily and
prepared for further flight.

But whither should they fly? No doubt could be
entertained that the whole country was now over-
run by the Russian cavalry, so that they could only
hope to escape by something like a miracle.
Hortense consulted a map of the environs of Paris,
and determined on endeavouring by a circuitous
route to reach Trianon, where she might for a while
at least be protected by General Préval, then
stationed with a considerable body of troops at

Versailles. While she was discussing with her attendants the means of flight, the explosions of
artillery came constantly booming on the night air,
making her heart sick. She had never before heard
the report of a great gun, except during the cele-
bration of military fêtes, and her imagination was
not sufficiently active to carry her to those many
cities, which, while she reposed in luxury and indo-
lence, had been attacked, and battered down by
Napoleon to gratify the passion of the French for
glory. As I have said, the roar of the cannon made
her heart sick now. She trembled for her children,
she trembled for herself, and preparations were made
for instant departure.

On arriving at Le Petit Trianon, General Prèval
waited on the queen, but brought her no intelligence
about what was going on in Paris. The artillery
still thundered, and they knew, therefore, that the
Parisians were holding out. At length the firing
ceased, and though it was altogether uncertain which
party had been victorious, her gaiety in some measure
returned to her. Presently a soldier was seen approaching through the long avenue from Versailles.
One of the ladies in waiting ran to meet him. "What
news?" she exclaimed. "That," he replied, " is
what I am ordered to inform the queen alone."

When he had delivered his message, Hortense called
for the first gentleman in waiting, and ordered the
horses to be put to her carriage, because they must
depart instantly. The gentleman replied, that supposing her majesty would sleep at Trianon, the men
servants had gone to Versailles. " And yet I had
ordered them," she said quietly, " to remain here
with me. However, let all who are within call be
brought together, for we must set out at once.
General Prèval has sent to inform me that the French
troops have evacuated Versailles, together with all
the environs of Paris, and are in full retreat towards
the south; the kings, Joseph and Jerome, have just
passed through the town, on their way to join Marie
Louise. The allies are masters of Paris, and foreign
soldiers will in all likelihood be here presently. With
the utmost speed we can make, therefore, we shall
barely be able to keep up with the last skirts of the
rear guard. My desire is that we may sleep to-night
at Rambouillet."

Through the exertion of much energy, everything
was speedily got ready. They set out, and reaching
Rambouillet at a very late hour, found the kings at
supper, and the ministers all huddled together in the
ante-chamber, making antics and grimaces to keep
their courage up. Their traditional politeness had

entirely left them, kings and all; for instead of ex-
erting themselves to aid the queen in her flight, or
even expressing the slightest sympathy for her forlorn
condition, they only augmented her terrible anxieties,
by observing coolly, that if she could not obtain the
means of immediately pursuing her journey, she
would probably, together with her sons, be taken
prisoners that very night by the Cossacks. They
themselves had engaged all the horses at Rambouillet,
so that nothing was left for her but to take her
chance. She had, as usual, seen the children safe in
bed. Fatigue had probably taken away their appetite, which was fortunate; since neither kings nor
ministers offered them anything to eat. One of the
principal ladies of her retinue considered herself
lucky to obtain from a friend a crust of bread,
which she bore off in triumph to her bedroom. Late
in the night, loud voices were heard in the ante-
room, and apprehensions of the Cossacks revived.
It turned out only to be a French colonel, who commanded the last regiment in the rearguard, and expected to find the minister of war at Rambouillet.
The queen saw this swearing colonel, and told him
that since the minister of war had fled, she ordered
him to remain there all night with his regiment to
protect her and her children. When morning came,

however, it was found that the gallant colonel had followed the example of the minister of war, and disappeared with his men during the night, leaving the queen and her sons to whatever mercy there might be in the Cossacks, should they happen to come up.

As usual, poor Louis, ex-king of Holland, contrived maladroitly, by his messengers, to prevent his wife from enjoying a wink of sleep. No sooner had she got into bed, than an officer came from him with a letter, ordering her—for he had become imperative during his troubles—to join him and the Empress Marie Louise at Blois. The patience of Hortense at length gave way. "I had intended," she said, " to go to Blois, but now I won't!" Then sitting up in bed in her night dress, she wrote three letters, one to her husband, another to Marie Louise, and a third to the emperor. Presently three ladies of rank, trembling fugitives from Paris, came in, fatigued, dejected, and so hungry, that they were glad to share Mdlle. Cochelet's crust.

I have said that Hortense had resolved to disobey her husband, and instead of proceeding to Blois, to take refuge with her mother Josephine, at the château of Navarre, in Normandy. Despair often gives people courage. Though the enemy might at any

moment arrive, she exhibited a certain amount of
tranquillity. By degrees morning broke, the carriages
came, and the queen, taking leave of such of her
friends as were destined for Blois, entered, to the
surprise of every one, the forest of Rambouillet.
But she was prudent in her very imprudence. As
M. D'Arjuzon, the only gentleman of the party, was
unacquainted with that part of the country, she had
taken along with her a garde champêtre, to lead the
way through the woods.

They had advanced but a short distance, when a
servant came riding up full speed, to say that the
Cossacks were already, at four o'clock in the morning,
scouring over a neighbouring plain.   It appeared probable, moreover, that they had likewise entered the
forest; nothing now was left for the queen but to
strike into the great road to Maintenon, on which she
overtook a multitude of fugitives, making the best of
their way, bag and baggage, towards the provinces.
They had not advanced a quarter of a league, before
one of the dreaded Russian horsemen galloped out
of the forest, with his long whip in his hand.   The
queen's single outrider, being a gallant fellow, dashed
furiously towards him, upon which he re-entered the
wood, but presently appeared again with another
Cossack.   Deceived, however, by the multitude of

fugitives, who seemed to be advancing towards them in one compact body, they judged it prudent to retreat, and the queen arrived unmolested at Maintenon.

Here she found a regiment of cavalry, from the commander of which she obtained an escort; and then proceeded by a cross road in much greater safety towards Louis, the château of M. D'Arjuzon, who had kindly invited her to pass a night there. Every incident of this journey combined to augment the alarm of Hortense for the safety of her children. Whether she considered the circumstances of the country she had left, or of that she was now entering upon, her perplexity was increased. Scarcely had she quitted Maintenon, when she met a courier from the emperor, who informed her that he was advancing with his army upon Paris. Shortly afterwards, she arrived at a village, whose inhabitants were greatly alarmed at the appearance of her escort, which they mistook for the advanced guard of the enemy. In truth, the allied troops were now dispersed in smaller or greater bodies over all that part of France, and the fears of the poor villagers were in a few hours fully realised.

It is highly probable that had the Cossacks been able to foresee that the boy of six years old, of whom they were now in pursuit, would in the course of a few years be Emperor of the French, they would have displayed much greater eagerness for his capture. For the moment, however, all that part of the country enjoyed the most delightful tranquillity, and they travelled through shady lanes, and among the windings of beautiful vallies, which presented an exquisite picture of pastoral life. They arrived late at Louis, and here the queen, believing herself to be in safety, dismissed her escort.

CHAP. V.

THE CHÂTEAU OF NAVARRE.

NEXT morning, at five o'clock, they set out in fearful weather, and through extremely bad roads,
towards the château of Navarre. On reaching her
mother's residence, Hortense found herself evidently
with no small surprise in the midst of royalists, who
looked on her arrival as a sinister event. It is not
quite clear that Josephine herself greatly rejoiced at
it. She embraced her daughter and her grandsons,
but exhibited her old weakness for people of rank,
who belonged to the ancient régime. The whole
country was in commotion. Napoleon had given
orders that all the strong places in the provinces
should put themselves in a state of defence; but the
energies of the nation were exhausted, and notwithstanding the turbulence of its feelings, experienced
very little inclination to prolong the contest with the
allies.

The situation of Hortense and her two sons at
Navarre was not altogether pleasant. Josephine was

weak and capricious, sometimes giving way to absurd lamentations, sometimes endeavouring to spoil her daughter's children. She was particularly partial to the younger one, Louis, whose countenance, she said, reminded her of her own daughter's in childhood. If there existed any resemblance out of her imagination, it is quite clear that Hortense never could have been beautiful. It is difficult to conceive a greater contrast than that presented by Josephine and Hortense. The mother, capricious, timid, weak, fond of gaiety, and pleasure, was little better than a Sybarite; while the daughter, firm, resolute, adventurous, full of energy and courage, was both in principle and practice a Spartan. She had a profound faith in the destinies of her house, and wished to prepare her sons from their childhood to play a distinguished part in the world.

It is not my intention to follow in this narrative the fortunes of the Bonaparte family, or to allude, except very briefly, to what regards the emperor. After the capitulation of Paris, he went to Elba, where he amused himself with acting royalty on a small scale.

Very different accounts are given of the financial condition of Josephine and Hortense. The former, always thoughtless and extravagant, found herself, on the fall of Napoleon, overwhelmed with enormous debts. Hortense, on the contrary, had preserved her diamonds from the wreck of her fortunes, and having taken them along with her, resolved to sell them, and live on the proceeds. Others say, and not apparently without reason, that all the Bonaparte family had contrived to secrete wealth, and to distribute it nearly over the whole of Europe. This is the more probable view, when we consider what afterwards took place. But it will be better to discuss this subject further on in the narrative.

At this time Hortense had to choose between remaining in France to share the fortunes of her house, and retiring to some foreign country, where she might live in peaceful affluence. The family of her mother possessed an estate in the island of Martinique, and her plan at this time was to go and settle in that island. She hated her husband, with whom she had always lived on the worst possible terms, and her principal fear now was that he would take her sons from her.

While in this state of doubt and perplexity, she was informed by a letter from Paris that the emperor Alexander took much interest in her fate, and had caused an article to be inserted in the treaty of Fontainebleau, securing to her complete authority over her

sons during their youth. It would be necessary,
therefore, for her to remain in France, and she was
strongly urged by her friends to return without delay
to Malmaison, where she might deliberate, in conjunction with the Czar, on the future interests of her
children. No explanation has been given of the
policy pursued by Alexander towards Hortense at this
period. He was a man of generous and susceptible
nature, and may have been warmed into enthusiasm
by the accounts he had heard of her beauty, devotion, and maternal tenderness. At any rate, he
expressed to one of her ladies his intention of going
down himself to' the château of Navarre, should
Hortense find it impracticable to perform the journey
to Paris.

The character of this prince is one of the most
curious in modern history. In the midst of numerous weaknesses which constantly made him the plaything of fanatics or impostors, he exhibited several
qualities of a strong mind, judged of men and things
for himself, and judged correctly, cherished an extraordinary admiration for the genius of Napoleon, and
yet, in conjunction with England, effected his overthrow. In the intervals between his fits of ambition
he delighted to pass his time in the society of women,
to surround himself with the elements of romance,

and to succumb to the influence of a gentle melancholy, which was often succeeded by bursts of passionate resentment.

For some reason or another Hortense was at this time considered separately from the Bonaparte family, perhaps because she no longer lived with her husband. She had made a strong impression on a number of persons who were all anxious to serve her, but desired in the first place that she should return immediately to the capital. At an interview which one of her ladies had with the emperor Alexander, he inquired respecting the possessions of Hortense, and particularly about the château and grounds of St. Leu. Having ascertained that they were a sort of family apanage, he observed that they must be settled on her as her own exclusive property, and said he would cause Count Nesselrode to make the necessary arrangements for erecting St. Leu into a duchy.

" Blacas," he added, " will then get the King's signature to the document, and you must persuade the queen to agree to it. The affairs of Eugéne Beauharnais and the empress Josephine have been easily settled, but there is more difficulty respecting the queen on account of the name borne by her sons. If nothing fixed and positive be established for them,

the Bourbons, I fear, would be capable of taking
away from her all she has; whereas by creating a
duchy, the possession of which the king shall make
over to her by his sign manual, such a result would
be rendered impossible, since they must respect a
grant guaranteed by me and all the allies."

The opinion entertained of the Bourbons by the
allied sovereigns and their ministers was anything but
flattering; they appear, observed Count Nesselrode,
to have come back from the other world, and to
be very much surprised that the children they left
at the breast a quarter of a century ago should
now be grown up to men and women.

Their folly, however, was not the worst trait
in their character. Like our Stuarts, they indulged
an impotent vindictiveness, which betrayed them into
acts of malice infinitely petty. When Hortense's
first child died in Holland, Napoleon, then in the
zenith of his power, caused the body to be conveyed
to Paris, and interred in the church of Notre Dame.
The proceeding was at once vain and impolitic,
because, if he desired the family of his brother Louis
to take root in the Dutch soil, he should have
begun the process by mingling with that soil the
ashes of its early dead. However, he had, like other
men, his weaknesses, and this was one of them.

But when the Bourbons returned, their keen-scented bigotry, legal and religious, speedily discovered that the remains of a Bonaparte had been deposited in the national cathedral. An article was immediately inserted in one of the journals, under the inspiration of the court, stating that the coffin was to be disinterred, and removed to one of the cemeteries of Paris. When Hortense was told of this act of Louis le Désiré, so becoming the descendant of a hundred kings, she observed coldly, " So much the better ! I shall claim the body of my child, and place it where it will be near me in the church of St. Leu." The coffin, having been dug up out of the hallowed earth of Notre Dame, was delivered to her, and she caused it to be again buried at St. Leu, where her sons Napoleon and Louis used, like good little Catholics, to kneel on the marble pavement, and pray for the soul of their departed brother.

CHAP. VI.

HORTENSE AND THE EMPEROR ALEXANDER.

It would be beside my purpose to describe the intercourse between the Emperor Alexander and Queen Hortense. The politics and the gaieties of Paris ceased to have any charm for him; he was perpetually at Malmaison; conversations with Josephine, with Eugène Beauharnais, with the children, now appeared to possess for him irresistible attractions. His mind, it was evident, had been thrown into a state of impassioned effervescence, such as he had once before experienced under the potent influence of Madame de Krudener. During this period of illusion, a party was made up to visit the water works at Marly. It was one of the characteristics of Hortense, to which I have already more than once alluded, that she could enjoy nothing without the presence of her children. On this occasion she led her eldest son by the hand, while the younger found himself under the united care of the Czar Alexander, and her brother Eugène.

They walked about, they laughed, they talked, they saw everything, they understood nothing, as is always the case with persons who are possessed by one absorbing idea.

'At length Alexander, in a state of complete abstraction, approached so near one of the great wheels, that in another instant he would have been caught by the skirts of his coat, whirled into the air, and dashed to pieces, together, perhaps, with the child whom he still held by the hand. Perceiving the danger, Hortense with a loud shriek, which made every one present tremble, rushed forward and pushed him away. Whatever might have been his inward emotions, he seems to have said little at the time, his attention having been directed towards the queen, whose excitement and alarm were extreme. However, he probably did not forget, that if she owed him her duchy, he owed her his life.

It has often been observed that children who are kept from other children, and live habitually with grown up persons, are what is called forward, and appear to have more sense than children in general of the same age. But nothing whatever is gained by this, for the progress they make when so young is altogether lost afterwards. Indeed, it has often been suspected that the mind rather loses than gains

strength by premature development. Under the
care of Hortense, Louis Napoleon and his brother
were transformed very early into something like
little men. One of her attendants remarks, that
they were really above their age in many respects,
which arose from the care taken by their mother to
form their characters and develope their minds.

They were, nevertheless, too young to comprehend
the nature of the new and striking events which
took place around them. Having been accustomed
to see no other kings or emperors but those of their
own family, they inquired naturally enough, when
the King of Prussia and the Emperor of Russia
were announced, if these also were their uncles, and
to be so addressed by them. " No," their attendants
replied, " you are simply to call them ' sire.' " " But
in point of fact," inquired Napoleon, " are they
not my uncles?" He was informed that all the kings
they now saw, so far from being their uncles, had
entered France as conquerors. " Then," replied the
elder boy, " they are the enemies of the emperor,
my uncle; why do they embrace us ?" " Because
this emperor of Russia, whom you see daily, is a
generous enemy, who desires to be of service to you
as well as to your mamma. But for him you
would possess nothing in the world, while your

uncle's condition would be far worse than it is."
" Then we must love him," replied the boy. " Yes,
certainly, for you owe him gratitude."

The younger prince Louis, who in general spoke very
little, had listened in silence, and with great attention
to this conversation. The next time Alexander came,
he took a little signet ring which his uncle Eugène had
given him, and approaching the emperor on tiptoe,
that he might attract no attention to his movements,
he gently slipped the ring into the emperor's hand,
and then ran hastily away. His mother called him
to her, and inquired what he had been doing. " I
had nothing but that ring," he replied, blushing and
hanging down his head; " my uncle Eugène gave it
to me, and I wished to give it to the emperor,
because he is good to mamma." The emperor
Alexander embraced the boy, and putting it on the
ring which held the bunch of seals suspended to his
watch, said, with emotion, that he would wear it for
ever.

In persons who possess a commanding position in
the world, there is no more certain means of success
than the habit of giving. Louis Napoleon seems
always to have acted upon this conviction. At
first doubtless it was a generous instinct, which was
afterwards cultivated by policy. When he was

much older, his mother one day reproached him, with giving away something which she had bestowed on him as a present. "Mother," he replied, "you meant I am sure to afford me pleasure by presenting it to me, and I have now had two pleasures, first that of receiving it from you, and then that of giving it to another."

The emperor Alexander and the other foreign sovereigns, then in Paris, when they saw the young princes daily at Malmaison, addressed them as Monseigneur, or your Imperial Highness, which greatly astonished the boys, who had never been used to that sort of jargon.

It was one great wish of their mother to preserve them from being puffed up by the circumstances of their position. People about them were requested to use, in speaking to them, the terms of affection and friendship, and to set ceremony aside. They used to say, "My little Napoleon, or my little Louis;" which accustomed them to greater simplicity than is usually found among princes. This no doubt produced a permanent effect upon their characters, and enabled Louis Napoleon afterwards to make himself popular among all classes. Hortense endeavoured to persuade them that greatness in itself was nothing, and that their real value consisted in what they themselves

were worth.   She often took them both on her
knees, and talked with them for the purpose of forming their ideas on all subjects. The conversation was
curious, during that period of splendour when they
were supposed to be the heirs of so many crowns,
which Napoleon lavished upon his brothers, his
relatives, and his generals. When she had questioned
them respecting what they already knew, she would
enlarge upon what they had still to learn, that they
might be equal to their own destiny, and know how,
in all conjunctures, to create themselves resources.

During the interval between the capitulation of
Paris and Napoleon's return from Elba, Hortense
was visited at St. Leu by numbers of remarkable
individuals, and among others, by Madame de Staël.
This woman was, no doubt, what is called a brilliant
talker, eaten up with vanity, eager for display, and
gifted with precisely those qualities and acquisitions
which enabled her to succeed in that design.

Having dazzled and bewildered everybody else, she
turned to the children, resolved apparently to extort
admiration even from them. But children form a world
apart, and require to be subdued by very different
arts from those which succeed with grown-up people.
She overwhelmed the young princes with questions,
she investigated, she made speeches, and at length

inspired them with intense ennui. "Do you love your uncle?" she inquired. "Very much." "Do you think you shall be as fond of war as he is?" "Yes, I should be, if it did not cause so much evil." " Is it true that your uncle often used to make you repeat the fable which begins with these words— 'The reason of the most powerful, is always the best?'" "Madame, he often used to make me repeat fables, but not that one oftener than any other." The younger Napoleon, who had a very superior mind, and a judgment beyond his age, replied to her with great calmness and circumspection, and when the affair was over, came to Madame Boubers, saying, "That lady is a great questionmonger; I wonder, now, if that is what people call genius?"

The occupations of Hortense, during the extraor- dinary period which separated Napoleon's abdication from the Hundred Days, were extremely varied. According to some accounts, she devoted her whole time to political intrigue; and, in conjunction with the partisans of the empire, organised those numerous plots and conspiracies, by which the mind of the French people was prepared for the reinstallation of Napoleon. I am not by any means interested in de- fending her from this charge, which, even if well- founded, exposes her, in my opinion, to no very just

censure.   But perhaps she did no more than excite,
in an indefinite way, the hopes of the Bonapartists
who thronged about her at St. Leu, where they naturally conversed chiefly of their regrets and anticipations.   As her wealth was considerable, she
indulged in something like indiscriminate hospitality.
All who had suffered by the restoration flocked
naturally to her house, which thus became the centre
of the disaffected.   The intelligence which reached
France from Elba, came directly to her, and she imparted to her friends just so much of it as seemed
calculated to produce a good effect.   The old
generals, the half pay officers, the political functionaries out of employment, the multitudinous agents of
the imperial government, who could extract nothing
from the Bourbons, turned their eyes towards St.
Leu, as the Muslims turn towards Mecca, in expectation that some ray of hope might at length break
upon them from thence.

But instead of enlarging on these subjects, I prefer
to contemplate her in her maternal character, which
the incidents of her sons' lives were often calculated
to bring out into strong relief.   All children have
teeth drawn, and suffer more or less during the operation.   But Louis Napoleon seems to have suffered,
on one occasion, more than the ordinary amount of

pain allotted to boys at such times. It often happens
that in drawing a tooth a small artery is ruptured,
and the hemorrhage thus caused would end in death,
if not arrested by art. Louis Napoleon seemed in
danger of passing out of life in this way. For two
days after he had his tooth drawn, he bled almost incessantly, until the attendants began to be alarmed.
His strength was nearly gone, and it was at length,
late in the night, determined that his mother ought to
be made acquainted with his state. On these occasions
she displayed much self-command, saying scarcely
anything, though it was easy to perceive, by her
countenance, how great was the anguish she felt.
By degrees the bleeding was stopped, and the child,
overcome by fatigue and exhaustion, fell into a profound sleep in his mother's arms. He was then laid
on the bed, and the nurse having been directed to
watch him, everybody else retired.

It was already one o'clock in the morning; the
queen had with all the others gone to rest, but was
unable to sleep, for the face of her child, pale and
covered with blood, rose perpetually before her.
Without waking any of her attendants, therefore,
she got up, threw a night dress over her, and, lamp in
hand, went into her child's room, where all was
silent and perfectly still. Both nurse and child

slept soundly; she drew near the bed without
desiring to wake the poor woman, who had been
quite exhausted by the fatigues of the evening.

She beheld her boy exactly as her fears had represented him, pale and bloody; she took him in her
arms, he did not wake, and his limbs fell, as if
without life. The blood gushed from between his
lips, and by instinct, rather than from thought, she
introduced one of her fingers into his mouth, and
pressed it hard on the wound. The blood stopped.
Fear almost arrested her breathing, but she in-
wardly thanked God for having incited in her the
thought of coming to her child, but for which he
would certainly have died. As for him, feeble and
fatigued, he continued to sleep, and from his breathing only, she perceived that he still lived. She
passed the whole night in this position, with her
finger pressed hard on his gums, without stirring or
calling any one, and by the morning scarcely a trace
remained visible of that wound which threatened at
one time to be so fatal.

The narrator of this anecdote exclaims, "Ah!
maternal love is the only real one in this world!"
It is in truth very powerful; but love in any form is
the same, and has given rise to nearly all the great

actions which shed a beauty and a glory on the history of mankind.

It may be worth mentioning, though the fact does not bear on Louis Napoleon, that his mother was extremely fond of violets, especially those of Parma, at that time rare in France, since they were nowhere cultivated except in the gardens of Malmaison, St. Cloud, and St. Leu. Every day the gardener was directed to forward to her a tin box filled with bouquets of violets and roses, which she distributed among the ladies who loved those flowers. For herself, her taste was so remarkable, that her entrance into the drawing-room immediately became known by the perfume of the violet diffused around her. In this partiality she resembled the Athenians, who were called the violet-crowned people.

CHAP VII.

ESCAPE AND CONCEALMENT.

ON the 6th of March, 1815, intelligence reached the French government, which deeply alarmed, and almost paralysed the whole Bourbon family. Throughout the winter, strong suspicions had settled, as I have observed, on Hortense, who was accused of being engaged in plots for the restoration of the imperial *régime*. On the day above named, she had been riding in the Bois de Boulogne, and was returning in her carriage down the Champs Elysées, and making for the bridge leading from the Place de la Revolution, when she met Lord Kinnaird, who stopped her carriage, and asked her if she had heard the news; she inquired what news. He answered, that the emperor had disembarked on the coast of France. The queen became as pale as death.

"It is impossible!" she exclaimed. "Who can have told you a story so absurd?"

"What I tell you is true," replied his lordship.

"I have just learned the fact from the Duke of Orleans, who is immediately to set out after the Comte d'Artois, who left Paris during the night."

"Oh heavens!" she exclaimed, "What calamities are about to overwhelm the emperor, France, and ourselves!"

Lord Kinnaird was of the same opinion, and observed "that the measures of the government had been well taken, that large bodies of troops had been precipitated towards the coast, and that it must, therefore, be soon over with Napoleon."

It seems not to have occurred to his lordship that the soldiers might refuse to fight against their old commander, and that the larger the army sent against him, the stronger he would be. Hortense was still incredulous, but the idea by degrees made its way into her mind, especially when his lordship added that the whole court was in a state of confusion, and that the most vigorous measures were to be taken against the partisans of Napoleon.

As a mother, Hortense's first fears were for her children, and she inquired eagerly whether Lord Kinnaird thought that any danger was likely to befal them. "It is very probable," he replied, "that they will be seized and kept as hostages."

"Oh, God!" she exclaimed, her eyes filling with

tears, " to what dangers have I exposed them!" Then her thoughts changing rapidly, she added, "But no; the French nation will not suffer them to be harmed." " The populace," he replied, "will soon become furious; and as it is not to be doubted that they have continued true to the emperor, the probability is that they will cut off every Englishman in Paris." " No, no, believe nothing of the kind, the people are no longer what they were in 1793. However, if you feel the slightest uneasiness, bring your wife and family to my house. I have nothing to fear from the people, and offer it to you as an asylum. But I am afraid of what the government may do to my children, and must return home immediately to watch over them." Lord Kinnaird then left her to look after his own family, and she hastened back to her palace.

It was resolved that her two sons should leave home at once, and go into a place of concealment, where she hoped they would be safe. The plan of fight was arranged, and all the necessary steps were taken for carrying it into execution. It so happened that she was on that very evening to have a large party at her house; that a celebrated singer had been invited, and that a number of her friends who were or professed to be fond of music were coming to

hear the performance. Should she put off this party
or not? How could she bear to assemble around
her a joyous and festive throng, while Napoleon on
the one hand, and the friends of the Bourbons on
the other, were perhaps at the very moment engaged
in mortal combat, and while French blood might be
shedding like water? She might even be suspected
of holding this gathering to celebrate the emperor's
landing. On the other hand, the intelligence was
not yet known to the public, and was only circulated
cautiously among the members of the government,
and the higher aristocracy.

If she seemed to be acquainted with the news, she
might be suspected of being in communication with
the emperor, and thus augment the animosity of the
Bourbons against both herself and her family. It was
determined, therefore, that whatever might be the
heaviness of her heart, she should endeavour to appear gay, and go through her social duties as if nothing
had happened. The guests assembled, — the music
and the singing commenced, and the majority of those
present exhibited the joyousness of ignorance, but on
some few faces there was a cloud; and Hortense,
therefore, could not refrain from suspecting that the
news had already begun to spread.

The hour fixed for the departure of her children

had not yet arrived, and she trembled every moment lest the agents of the government should appear to seize and snatch them from her; she could not even be sure that among the persons present there might not be some, secretly connected with the Bourbons and commissioned to watch her movements.

As soon as night had fairly set in, one of the ladies about Hortense went to the apartment of the young princes, and taking them by the hand, led them down softly to the garden; the nurse of the younger, who never quitted him, following close behind with a bundle of clothes. The valet had been despatched for a hackney coach, which was directed to wait for them at a considerable distance from the house. They passed out cautiously through the garden into the Rue Taitbout, where the elder boy inquired, "Whither are you taking us? Why must we be concealed? Is it that some danger threatens us, and if so, must mamma remain exposed to it?" "No, prince," replied his companion; "it is you and your brother only that are in danger; your mamma need fear nothing." "Oh, very well," he said, and went away quietly.

Hortense had given strict orders that they should not be told of the disembarkation of their uncle; but left in complete ignorance whither and for what reason

they were taken away. They, however, were delighted with the mystery of being hurried out through
a garden door, taken to a distance in the dark street,
put into a coach, and cautioned against making the
slightest noise.

This last injunction was rather irksome to the elder
brother, who loved talking; but the younger, naturally
silent and reserved, no doubt had his propensity
strengthened by the events of his childhood.   For a
long while, to speak freely would have endangered
him; he therefore acquired early the command of his
tongue, and to this habit, perhaps, owed much of his
future success.   When the lady returned, she made
a sign to the queen that all was well, and this appeared
to remove a great weight from her mind.

The reader who takes an interest in the subject of
this memoir, will not refuse to extend a portion of
it to his mother, who, at the time of which I am now
speaking, watched over him, like a domestic providence.   When she had done all she could to provide
for the safety of her children, it became necessary
for her to think of her own.   To remain in her
palace was judged by all her friends in the highest
degree imprudent; she also must fly, and conceal herself.   There was a lady at that time in Paris who,
together with her husband, owed everything to

Hortense, and she was justified, therefore, in supposing that this person would be but too happy to afford her an asylum for a few days. Attended by one female servant, she secretly quitted the palace at nine o'clock in the evening, and repaired on foot to her friend's house. What was her surprise, on being informed that she could not remain there longer than that night. Disgusted and angry, she left early in the morning, and returned at all hazards to her own residence.

But those who loved her became so anxious for her safety, that she was at length persuaded to disguise herself, and seek another asylum. She therefore put on the cloak, bonnet, and veil of her female reader, Mdlle. Cochelet, and, escorted by that young lady's brother, again went out on foot in search of a temporary home.

This time, instead of seeking the protection of any great personage, she brought down her ambition to the level of her brother's old nurse Mimi, who had accompanied Josephine from Martinique, and had been secured a small but comfortable independence by her old mistress. At every step she ran new risks. All day long men had been seen watching at the corner of the Boulevards, and parading up and down the street opposite her house. Her dis-

guise was incomplete, for underneath her cloak
she wore a magnificent dress of fine Indian muslin,
with open embroidery and trimmings of rich lace.
If any one in the street should catch a glimpse of
such a dress, she would be lost.   On occasions like
these, however, so little was she mistress of herself,
that the idea of going out alone with a young man,
contrary to all the etiquette of the imperial family,
appeared to her so ludicrous, that she burst into a
fit of laughter which she could scarcely restrain. Her
momentary protector was so alarmed by her indiscretion that he hardly knew what he was doing.

Nevertheless, she reached Mimi's apartments in
safety; and as that good woman happened to have
some visitors coming to her in the afternoon,
Hortense was stowed away in a sort of lumber
room, entered on one side by a little door, and on
the other by a hole in the wall.   Here she appeared
to be in safety, and at night was visited by her
female reader, who brought her the news.   She
soon, however, made a discovery which disquieted
her considerably.   In one of the lower floors of the
house lived a man who had formerly been aide-de-
camp to General De Broc, but who had now become
a fierce Bourbonist.   By his new patrons he had
been placed at the head of a division of the secret

police, to the members of which he gave audience daily in an apartment adjoining Hortense's lumber room.

Paris always abounds in strange approximations; but nothing more curious can well be imagined than the concealment of a queen in a garret, in the immediate vicinity of those who were employed by the government to hunt down and capture both her and her children. In this retreat Hortense, it may easily be supposed, received few visitors; but Alexandre de Giradin, an ardent partisan of the Bonaparte family, was one day brought thither by a lady of her suite. Having ascended floor after floor, M. de Giradin began to feel uneasy as he penetrated into the darker and more suspicious parts of the house; and when he approached the hole in the wall, through which it was necessary to crawl on all fours, he hesitated, and for a moment refused to proceed.

A loud laugh from Hortense soon put his timidity to flight. He descended into the dusky room, and conversed with her for a considerable time on the business about which he came; he told her that the Bourbons, more especially the Duc de Berri, suspected her of having conducted the conspiracy which had led to the return of Napoleon, and that she was sought for with the utmost vigilance and perseverance. The government, in fact, had determined to arrest all persons connected with the Bonaparte family, but these had succceded so well in concealing themselves, that the chief of the police declared before the council that they had defeated all his arts, and were nowhere to be found. This circumstance is highly honourable to the French character.

CHAP VIII.

EPISODE OF THE HUNDRED DAYS.

IT would be beside my purpose to describe in detail the events of those agitated and exciting times. Hortense was delivered from confinement by the entrance of Napoleon into Paris, and his reinstallation in the Tuileries, on the 20th of March. The French are a people full of enthusiasm, which in general, however, is not long lived. They effervesce in a moment, and soon become flat again. But for Napoleon, the attachment of the lower orders was genuine. They felt he had done much for France, and not being able to comprehend his motives, imagined it had been done for them. On his return from Elba, therefore, their joy knew no bounds. But among the upper classes, the feeling was different. They knew, as was acknowledged by the Duke of Vicenza, that the country was too much exhausted to repel a second invasion of the allies, and dreaded the consequences which this wild paroxysm of ambition must inevitably bring upon the community.

F

I have frequently observed that Hortense was never happy without her children, and therefore, on the very day of Napoleon's return, she sent to bring them from their retreat. The messenger found them playing and gambling about, perfectly ignorant, and careless of the political bustle of the world. The fortnight which had been so full of anxiety and disquietude for their mother and her friends, had been quite a holiday to them. No lessons, no themes, no Latin, — what a glorious state of idleness ! _ They learned with pleasure, however, that they were now to see their mother and their uncle. They could very well do without the Abbé Bertrand and the Latin grammar. Wrestling, leaping, sommersets had supplied the place of walking.

Meantime their mother had gone to the Tuileries, where she experienced much difficulty in approaching the emperor, through the vast crowd which surrounded him. When at length she came up, he embraced her coldly, and said, " Where are your children ? " " In concealment," she replied. " You have placed them," he observed, "in a false position in the midst of my enemies." It is not quite easy to see what he meant by these words, if they were really intended to be understood literally ; but as he always felt himself to be on the stage, the whole was probably a piece of acting.

On the following morning, Hortense, taking her two sons along with her, went early to the Tuileries. Napoleon received them with much tenderness, kissed them repeatedly, and kept them near him a long time. His own son being far away, he seemed desirous of lavishing upon his nephews those marks of affection which should have been his. He took them out to the balcony, and showed them with great pride to the people, who thronged beneath his windows. He carried them along with him also when he went to review the troops on parade, which of course afforded the boys extraordinary gratification. All Paris was intoxicated with joy. The regiment of Labedoyère, and a battalion of the imperial guard, had bivouacked on the Place du Carrousel, and the hearts of the Parisians leaped with delight as they beheld once more those old soldiers of Austerlitz, whose manly faces had now been doubly browned by the sun of the south.

Some few traits in Napoleon's character, which became visible at this time, may be worth mentioning briefly. The Bourbons and their ministers, having fled from Paris in extreme haste, had left behind them in the office for foreign affairs a treaty

between England, France, and Austria, against
Russia, which, to conciliate the emperor Alexander,
Napoleon caused to be shown to the Russian envoy
then in Paris. But Alexander despised the
Bourbons too much to take offence at any new act
of baseness on their part, and was not at all the
more disposed to tolerate the dangerous ambition of
the Corsican.

Josephine meanwhile had died, and Napoleon
went to visit her daughter at Malmaison. He is
said to have been much moved at the sight of her
bedroom; but this is scarcely reconcileable with a
remark he let fall during the same visit. Going
through the gallery with Denon, he appeared to be
struck by the beauty of the pictures, and inquired
how much they were worth. When the keeper of
the gallery had informed him, he observed, apparently half murmuring to himself, "Had I known
they were so valuable, I would never have given
them to Josephine." He then ordered them to be
purchased for the public gallery of the Louvre.

No man understood better than Napoleon the
effect of grand spectacles on the mind of the people.
He had kept his hold on the French nation, in a
great measure, by interesting their imaginations,
partly by his military exploits, partly by the grand

monuments he erected, partly by the dazzling shows
he caused to be exhibited before them. He now
believed, that what had succeeded during twenty
years could not altogether have lost its charm. He
projected, therefore, a magnificent ceremony, called
the Champ de Mai, which took place seventeen days
before the battle of Waterloo. But his piercing
eye must have beheld in everything around him
proofs that the old spirit of the French had departed,
that he had outlived the magic influence of his name,
and entered upon a new era, in which everything
was changed. It would be easy to call up before
the fancy a gorgeous picture of this ceremony. I
have myself been present in the Champ de Mars, when
one hundred and twenty thousand soldiers, animated
by the revolutionary spirit, have defiled, with the
pride of a new age, before republican generals.

Great preparations had been made for the cele-
bration of this ceremony, which may be called the
consecrating of the colours of the army. At one
end of the Champ de Mars had been erected a lofty
platform supporting a throne for Napoleon, and
behind it a sort of tribune for Hortense and her
sons. In front of the throne was an altar, upon the
steps of which stood the bishops, who were to offi-
ciate in the blessing of the colours. The weather

was beautiful, and the summer sun threw down
floods of light upon long lines of golden eagles,
which, as they moved in the hands of the standard
bearers, reflected the glittering rays on all sides.
The deputies of the people and the superior officers
of the army surrounded the emperor, while the
multitude extended in every direction in vast waves
towards the city, the country, and the river. It
was in some sense a new imperial election. A
writer, who stood that day among the crowd,
says that joy was universal, at least among the
people. This, I think, may be doubted. No one
then present could be ignorant that the armies
of all Europe were at that very moment gathering
together on the French frontier, preparing to dash
that imperial phantom to the earth, to disperse into
thin air the power he had erected on the fame of a
hundred battles, and to bring once more devastation
and slaughter to the very heart of Paris. Their
affection for Napoleon may have been still unshaken,
but their confidence in his fortune had departed,
never to return again.

It would be useless, therefore, to dwell on the
theatrical exhibitions by which he sought to re-
kindle their enthusiasm. He did his best, and they
did their best; but the play had been played out,

and nothing remained to be done but to drop the
curtain on the imperial pageant, and let the world
enjoy, as well as it could, the farce after the tragedy.
It is unnecessary to dwell on the battle of Waterloo.
It was fought; Napoleon lost it, and returned forthwith to Paris, with the conviction deep in his heart,
that everything in this world was over for him. He
had burnt down life's candle to the socket, and in
hastening to extinction, it began to make an unpleasant smell in the nostrils of the bystanders, and in
his own too. Not a spark of energy was left in him,
and he went to conceal with Hortense at Malmaison
the last remnant of the shame and agony of defeat.

Now it was that the character of this woman
shone forth in all its lustre. Every act of her life
had proved her to be a fond and good mother,
watchful in her tenderness, indefatigable in her
affection, ready at any moment to jeopardise her
own life for her sons. But her attachment for
Napoleon, especially now that he was in irremediable
affliction, rose above everything, and she determined
to hide her children, that she might give up for the
moment all her care and attention to him.

Many persons of opulence and distinction offered
to take charge of the boys; but not desiring to compromise them with the Bourbons, or for other

motives which may easily be divined, she preferred
trusting them to the care of Madame Tessier, an
honest hosier on the Boulevard Montmartre.   When
this resolution had been come to, she sent for the
valet-de-chambre of her elder son, and for the nurse
of the younger, and told them to get everything
ready immediately for taking the children to a safe
place of concealment.   Hortense, however, did not
relinquish to them the care of these preparations, but
presided over everything herself, and when all was
ready, left them the necessary directions, and set out
during the night for Malmaison to receive the
emperor in the morning.

The nurse of Prince Louis, who has already been
mentioned several times, was a Madame Bure, whose
name deserves to be recorded for her strong attachment to her charge.   Her mild and affectionate
character caused her to be beloved by the whole
household; she was a small, pretty brunette.   One
day when she went with the young prince to the
Tuileries, Napoleon, fixing his eyes upon her face,
exclaimed, " That young rogue has a very charming
nurse ! "

The writer who relates this anecdote observes,
with much simplicity, that these words of the emperor excited the only ebullition of vanity which

Madame Bure experienced during her whole life ; if so, she must have been the very black swan celebrated by Juvenal. Her affection for the young prince was that of a tender mother, and constituted the strongest feeling of her life. Wherever he went, she accompanied him, and many years afterwards she formed a part of the queen's household at Arenenberg, where she was always treated with peculiar kindness and attention; a fact which is equally honourable to all parties.

Napoleon at this time gave abundant proofs that the energy of his character was at length exhausted. His genius was extinguished, his imagination collapsed, and he sank at once into a state of hopeless weakness. He had really in some sort been the embodiment of the revolutionary spirit, and was kept up in his artificial elevation by the effervescing passions of the French people. Those passions had now subsided, and he ceased at once to be a hero. On the 24th of June, six days after the battle of Waterloo, he quitted Paris, never more to return, and proceeded to Malmaison, whither, as I have said, Hortense had repaired on the preceding night to receive him.

All who took any interest in Napoleon, or in her, were alarmed by the sinister reports, every hour put

into circulation. It was rumoured that 200 Bourbonists, full of fanaticism and brutality, had set out
for Malmaison to assassinate the emperor and the
queen, and a lady who had just returned to Paris
related that she had met these miscreants on the
road on horseback, and fully armed. A messenger
was therefore despatched to put the intended victims
on their guard. Meanwhile, the Bourbonists in
Paris believed themselves to be exposed to still
greater dangers. The people, it was feared, would
rise and renew the massacres of 1793. The nobility,
therefore, shut their gates and their windows, and
kept themselves secluded in the back rooms of their
houses.

It forms no part of my purpose to describe the
scenes which now took place at Malmaison. Some
determined to go along with Napoleon, others bade
him an external adieu, and Hortense felt that she
and her sons must be among the latter. She therefore sent for them to take their leave. With much
timidity and circumspection, they were withdrawn
from the house of the hosier, on the Boulevard
Montmartre, put into a carriage, and driven by a
very round-about way to Malmaison.

Napoleon was pre-eminently deficient in sensibility. His thoughts, his feelings, his hopes, his

fears were concentrated upon himself. When taking
leave for ever of his mother, he merely said, " Farewell, mother," and she, " Farewell, my son." They
then embraced each other and parted, as if they
had been going on a short journey. From the
sons of Hortense, he is said to have separated with
more external tokens of regret, and it is related,
that the children cried much, and expressed a strong
desire to go away with him. However, on the 29th
of June, Hortense and her sons quitted Malmaison
for Paris.

The palace of Hortense had a terrace at the
bottom of the garden overlooking the Rue Taitbout, through which the carriages of the grandees
drove towards St. Denis to salute Louis XVIII.
Hortense stood on this terrace looking on, while
a number of royalists shouted and menaced her
fiercely. This frightened her attendants, who
earnestly entreated her to take refuge in the
house of some friend, and there to conceal herself till Paris should be somewhat tranquillised. To
this she at last consented, and the factotum of Count
Nesselrode, under the impression that she was a
Russian lady, took lodgings for her and her children
in the very Rue Taitbout where she had been so
lately threatened. By chance or contrivance, the

lodgings were taken on a floor overhead a celebrated Bourbonist, who could hardly be suspected of having a member of the Napoleon family so near him. It may be observed that the house was opposite a small gate leading out of her own palace.

Here she remained with her sons carefully se-cluded, and living, in fact, like a prisoner. July 6th, the day the allies entered Paris, one of the ladies of her court, who had always been most attached to her, went to give her some news of what was going on. She found Hortense sitting in a little garden in the interior court of the house, with the two boys playing about her. This garden was nearly twenty feet square, and formed the only play-ground for the young princes, who however contrived, even in that confined space, to take sufficient exercise, while their mother followed mechanically all their move-ments with her eyes. While the boys continued playing, her gossiping visitor sat down and related to her all the news in the utmost possible detail. The queen, having become extremely tired of her confine-ment, was easily persuaded to go out and take a turn about the city.

Leaving the boys at home, they went forth as completely disguised as possible and stationed the prince's valet far in the rear, with directions not to appear to belong to them. On arriving at the barrier, they beheld the English uniform, at which Hortense gave a deep sigh. On their return they encountered persons by whom they did not wish to be recognised, and rushing up to the first *porte cochère* they could see, knocked and rang. As soon as the porter opened the door, Hortense perceived Madame St. Martin, at sight of whom she rushed back, and ran out again into the street, her companion following her. The porter, of course, took them for a couple of mad women. At length they returned to the queen's retreat, tired and out of breath.

CHAP. IX.

GOING INTO EXILE.

THE events of the last few months had inspired
Hortense with a strong desire to leave France for
ever, and retire to Switzerland, where she might
watch in peace over the education of her sons.
Everything among our neighbours is accomplished,
more or less, through the instrumentality of women.
Mdlle. Ribout, who had always been much attached
to Hortense, now called on Fouché, Duke of Otranto,
and explained to him the queen's desire to obtain
passports. The Bourbons were always weak, vacillating, and tricky. Louis XVIII., in ordering the
passports to be given her, professed to look upon her
departure with regret, and said he acted under the
conviction that, in the present disturbed state of the
country, it might be advisable for her to retire for a
few months; but that she and her children might
then return with perfect safety.

But the Bourbons were never remarkable for

generosity. She was informed she might go, but
nobody told her with what funds. Her finances
had probably been thrown into disorder by recent
events, and she was therefore considerably at a loss
for ready money, and found herself under the necessity of selling her pictures and other objects of art,
in order to be able to travel in a suitable manner,
with her children. Among the purchasers who presented themselves was M. de Talleyrand, who obtained possession of one of her best pictures for sixteen
thousand francs. Who became masters of the others is
not stated, but with the proceeds of her gallery, she
soon found herself in a condition to commence her
journey.

On the 17th of July, 1815, M. Devaux, Hortense's
steward, received an order from Herr Muffling, the
governor of Paris under the allies, stating that she
must quit the city in two hours. The reason given
for so offensive a proceeding was, that she had been
concerned in a plot for assassinating all the foreign
princes then in the capital. Devaux represented to
Muffling that she could not leave in such haste, and
obtained a few hours' delay, but was informed that
she should not sleep within the walls that night, and
must therefore set out before dark. She was to be
escorted out of France by the Count de Voyna, aide-

de-camp to Prince Schwartzenburg*, and chamberlain
to the Emperor of Austria. Madame Nicolai, an old
friend, offered the queen her château near Paris, where
she might sleep the first night. The children were
brought from their hiding place, and while they were
preparing to start, all sorts of dark reports assailed
their ears. It was said that some Bourbonists intended lying in wait for them on the road, and
assassinating the whole party for the millions in jewels
and gold which they were supposed to have with
them. This threw the family into a state of terror.

One of two things must be said of Hortense on
this occasion : either that she had no time for acting
a part, or that the suddenness of her movements had
steeled her against everything, for she exhibited no
emotion on quitting her friends, who were all in tears
about her.

The few necessary preparations having been made,
Hortense quitted Paris at nine o'clock in the evening,
July 17th. She and her two sons travelled in one
carriage, M. de Marmold and the Comte de Voyna
in a Berlin, Louis Napoleon's nurse and the *femme-*

---

* M. Felix Wouters, in order, I suppose, to impart an ad-
ditional air of grandeur to Hortense's departure, says that
Schwartzenburg himself had the generosity to take her under
his protection, and accompany her to Switzerland! (14.)

de-chambre in a third carriage, and Vincent, her
eldest son's valet, rode in front as a courier. They
slept the first night at the château de Bercy, belong-
ing to Madame Nicolai, who received and treated
them with the utmost hospitality.

Nothing particular occurred till they arrived at
Dijon, which they reached about dusk. At the
hôtel, while the horses were being taken from her
carriage, a party of the royal guard came up, and
surrounded it, attracted, probably, by the vast sums
of money it was supposed to contain. Well-dressed
ladies collected, and cried out, " Vive le roi." The
Count de Voyna, leaving her at the hotel, went out
to purchase for himself a pair of spectacles, and
during his absence, several soldiers broke into her
chamber, and said they were ordered to arrest her in
the king's name. This they did with furious looks
and gestures, displaying their bravery by insulting a
woman. She replied, " Very well, gentlemen, I am
your prisoner," and drew her children close to her.
The Austrian soldier whom De Voyna had left to
protect her in his absence, ordered these insolent
Frenchmen out of the room, and during the dispute
De Voyna returned, upon which they were ejected
by main force. The row went on all night, the
heroic Frenchmen drinking, swearing, and strutting

G

to and fro, flourishing their sabres, and letting the
metal scabbards clink against the ground to make
more noise. But it was in vain they raged.
Foreigners, now their masters, were in the town; they
endeavoured to deceive the Austrians by prodigious
lies, but to no purpose. The queen was protected,
and passed out of the city, while the ladies who cried
" Vive le roi ! " complained that they were deprived of
this enjoyment by the Austrian soldiers. The royalist
general, in order to facilitate her escape, held a review early in the morning, and commanded all the
French soldiers in the place to be present at it,
which prevented any chance of collision between
them and the Austrians.

Beyond the last outposts of the army of occupation,
the peasants, when they knew it was Hortense who
was passing by, flocked in crowds about her carriage,
throwing bouquets into it, crying, "Vive l'Empereur,"
and saying, "that the good went away, while the
bad remained." This at least showed that Napoleon
was popular in that part of the country, as, in fact, he
was everywhere among the peasants.

At Dole, there was another rising, very different
from that of Dijon. The worthy people took it into
their heads that the Count de Voyna was carrying
the queen away prisoner, and wanted to kill him in

order to deliver her. An old man, who was spokesman for the rest, having listened attentively to the queen's explanation, that De Voyna was her friend, and that she was going with him voluntarily, replied, " I believe it : you have only to say one word." The rest was understood, and signified, " We will throttle M. de Voyna in a moment." The crowd at length dispersed, and Hortense arrived safely at Geneva.

Here she was astonished to find that the magistrates, either because they detested the Bonaparte family, or wished to ingratiate themselves with the new French government, would not allow her to settle in the canton, and she was ordered to quit next morning. De Voyna requested a few days' delay, that he might write to Paris, and learn what was to be done with her. At the inn where she stayed, a number of officers were to meet next day to celebrate Napoleon's overthrow, and as their proceedings could not have proved otherwise than offensive to her, De Voyna advised a short trip among the Alps; and in conformity with his advice, she set out early in the morning, taking her children along with her.

As you stand on the ramparts of Geneva, with your face towards Savoy, you behold an isolated and naked mountain, towering to a great height above the city, and forming, so to say, the vanguard of the mighty ridges which, retreating and ascending tier above tier, terminate in those snow-clad pinnacles, which appear to pierce and support the amethystine firmament. Directing her course towards Mont Salis, she proceeded as far as possible in her carriage; but the road soon terminating in a narrow winding pathway, she alighted, and continued to climb the mountain on foot. All around, nature wore a grand and rugged aspect. Rocks, gorges, glens, narrow defiles, and precipices succeeded each other rapidly, producing a new and powerful effect upon the mind. The path as they advanced became less and less distinct, but presently changed its character, and led over easy and pleasant slopes between neatly clipped hedges. Soon the rude air of the Alps began to be impregnated with the perfume of flowers, while marks of the hand of man were impressed everywhere upon the soil. At length Hortense perceived, perched high among the rocks, a little old man, very coarsely dressed, who, leaving his eyrie, descended slowly to meet them.

When she had explained who she was, he replied, that he had heard of her persecutions, and invited her to enter his dwelling, a small, quaint, odd little edifice, covered all over for warmth with the bark of trees. It had two rooms, a kitchen, and a sleeping

chamber, to the latter of which you ascended by a
ladder. The furniture of the house was as simple as
its structure; but the owner's looks and language
soon convinced Hortense that she was not in the
hovel of a peasant. By degrees the hermit became
communicative, and told her he had formerly been a
physician at Geneva, but that having, probably
through some unsuccessful affair of the heart, conceived a hatred of human society, he had retired to
this mountain, that he might be troubled as little as
possible by the presence of man. Still, as he was
too much of a Sybarite to attend altogether upon
himself, he had to endure the perpetual penance of
being accompanied by a servant.

This unhealthy minded old gentleman had carried
a few books along with him, and in his bedroom,
which was also his study, there stood a table with
materials for writing. If addicted to self-examination,
he might have written an excellent treatise on hypo-
chondriasis. From the neighbourhood of his cell, the
eye commanded a view, scarcely to be rivalled on the
surface of the globe. Far down lay the broad blue
waters of the lake, traversed by the arrowy Rhone,
and fringed all round by banks of emerald, thickly
dotted with towns and cities, with villages, hamlets,
churches, and romantic homesteads, closely embosomed

in trees; on the left rose the verdant summit of the
Jura, on the right the pinky snows of the Bernese
Alps.

On this scene I have looked from every possible
point of view ; from the canton of Geneva, from the
mountains of Savoy, from the summit of the Jura,
from Meillerie, from Vevay, from Lausanne, in
summer and in winter, in autumn and in spring —
and yet so grand, so varied, so replete with beauty
is the prospect, that it appeared to put on fresh charms
every hour, and to engrave itself on the imagination
and on the memory. As Hortense was a woman of
much sensibility, which at that moment was enhanced
by sadness, she could not have regarded this landscape
without a strong bounding of the heart. Her children
were, however, too young to share her feelings,
though her companions, an Austrian and a Frenchman, probably could.

Some days afterwards, Napoleon's mother, together
with her brother, Cardinal Fesch, arrived at Geneva,
on their way to Italy. They remained one day to dine
with Hortense, and then continued their route. The
members of this family were always possessed by so
concentrated a selfishness, that they could meet and
part with the greatest coolness. Letitia aped the
Spartan, and perhaps had very little trouble in putting

on the appearance of insensibility. The situation of her daughter-in-law at this time, exiled, friendless, and altogether uncertain respecting the practicability of settling anywhere, might otherwise have induced her to linger for a few days at Geneva, to afford her such consolation as her presence was calculated to impart. The idea in all likelihood never occurred to her. She was hastening to play the part of a second female pope at Rome, and therefore cared very little what Hortense and her boys had to undergo. Exactly the same remark may be applied to Cardinal Fesch. He had played out his game of advancement in France, and was impatient to make a new series of moves on a more contracted, though not for that reason a less exciting scene.

CHAP. X.

INCIDENTS AT AIX.

BEING compelled to leave Geneva, Hortense with her children went to Aix in Savoy, whence De Voyna returned to Paris, in order to serve her, though apparently without any result.   He was a young man of twenty, but as grave as a judge, and well fitted for diplomacy under Metternich.   Here Hortense took a house, which had attached to it a large court, where Louis Napoleon and his brother collected the little boys of the neighbourhood, and taught them to play at soldiers.   Louis was drummer, and marched at the head of the troop, making all the noise he could, while Napoleon with a tin sword was commander.

While her children were thus amusing themselves, Hortense was assailed by new troubles.   The system of reaction was developing itself rapidly, and in a fearful manner throughout the south.   Crimes against the partisans of the revolution became frequent ; Marshal Brune was assassinated at Avignon, and it came to the knowledge of the Austrian

general Rochemann, who commanded the allied
forces at Lyons, and in all the neighbouring provinces,
that the lives of Hortense and her sons were
menaced. He conceived it to be his duty to inform
her of this danger; but because a letter might compromise him, he despatched an aide-de-camp to Aix
to describe his apprehensions verbally. Observing
the delicate state of her health, the aide-de-camp
explained his mission, not to her, but to the Austrian
officer appointed to watch over her, and he confided
the secret to her female reader. As reports of
all kinds were at that time ripe in France, I know
not what amount of credit should be attached to
general Rochemann's communication It imported,
however, that by some occult authority in Paris,
which suspicion can hardly fail to point out, several
miscreants, armed with poignards, had been sent
to take off Napoleon's nephews, and thus diminish
the number of pretenders to the throne. It seems
perfectly certain that all members of the Bonaparte
family were strictly watched.

It was said that Joseph and Jerome had been
arrested in Switzerland, Lucien at Turin; and though
this rumour proved to be unfounded, no doubt was
entertained that they moved about perpetually with
emissaries at their heels, ready to seize upon the

slightest pretext for delivering them over to the vengeance of the restored dynasty. That they were hostile to the restoration is certain, that they plotted against it is more than probable ; but for a while terror rendered them prudent, and whatever, therefore, their designs may have been, they contrived to envelope them in a mystery too thick to be penetrated by the Bourbon police.

Such periods of history have always been marked by crimes; we know, from our own annals, that ruffians infuriated with loyalty, or the thirst of gold, were always ready and even eager, to imbrue their hands in the blood of those whom they regarded as the king's enemies. By assassins of this kind, inspired by political fanaticism, Dr. Dorislaus was murdered at the Hague, and Mr. Anthony Ascham at Madrid. Cromwell himself had been marked out for their daggers, and though they failed in their design, yet in all likelihood the perpetual terror in which a full knowledge of their flagitious purposes kept him, shortened his days.

Similar passions led to similar atrocities in France· Hortense, as I have already observed, had been expelled from Paris as an assassin, who contemplated the murder of all the allied sovereigns. Nothing is so suspicious as guilt. Her enemies thought her capable of such

a crime, because they themselves experienced no repugnance to perpetrate crimes equally heinous. Through
the humanity of those around her, however, she was
for a while spared the agony which the knowledge
of what was meditated against her sons would have
inflicted on her. All the members of her household
appear to have co-operated enthusiastically for the
preservation of her and her children, and that, too,
without suffering the slightest indication of their solicitude to be seen. No strangers were on any pretext admitted into the house. When she and the
children went out, they were accompanied and
watched over, not as if through the fear of any
special enemies, but merely as a measure of general
precaution. It may be fairly presumed, therefore,
that general Rochemann's kindness proved the
means of preserving the present ruler of the
French.

The allied governments exhibited extreme littleness
in all that related to the settlement of the Bonaparte
family. The residence of Hortense and her sons employed the serious deliberations of England, Russia,
Austria, Prussia, and France, which, while permitting
her to inhabit Switzerland, directed their ambassadors,
not only to watch strictly over her, but by their petty
intermeddling to embarrass all her movements. This

solicitude was obviously not so much aimed against
her as against her sons, who, when they should grow
up, might endanger the throne of the Bourbons.
While this subject was occupying her mind, a new
cause of vexation presented itself. Her husband
having determined to settle in the Roman States,
sent to Aix a certain Baron de Zuite with a peremptory demand that she should yield up to him her
eldest son. For some time she had expected that the
ex-king of Holland would take this step; but the
blow, though not unforeseen, was still severely felt.
She was fond of her children, and to part with one of
them under any circumstances was a misfortune, but
in the present case she looked upon it moreover as an
insult.

The Baron de Zuite was a person by no means
calculated to inspire an affectionate mother with
confidence. Any other woman, though less careful than she was, of their education and safety,
would have shrunk from confiding her son to such a
man. His countenance was truly the image of his
soul, indicating, in the most unmistakable manner,
the existence of every evil passion, and every vice.
It was difficult to imagine where King Louis could
have found such an individual, and, when he had met
with him, how he could think of sending him on such

a mission. The queen formed a very different judgment of the baron, and refused to entrust her son to his care. This, however, she did with much policy. She informed M. de Zuite that it would be wrong for him to set out without taking a little rest, that it would be better for him to make the acquaintance of her son before he set out with him, and to allow time for the tutor to arrive from Paris, whom she wished to accompany his charge into Italy. This preceptor was not a man distinguished for abilities; but his morality was indisputable, and that, under the circumstances, was the principal consideration. But Hortense did not become reconciled, by delay, to the idea of losing her son. The more she reflected upon it, the more it afflicted her, as appeared evident from the wasting away of her frame.

When people contemplate history from the orthodox point of view, they are apt to regard it as something very dignified. They persuade themselves that it has nothing to do with little people or little things, and that kings, emperors, and princes, are at once enlarged in their views, and generous and liberal in their appreciation of others. Experience teaches us that it is often quite otherwise. For example, Hortense, in quitting Paris, imagined she had delivered both the Bourbons and their allies from all violent apprehensions on her account. But Louis XVIII. and his ministers belonged to that class of persons who behold a bandit in every bush. Having been informed by their intelligent emissaries of the amusements of the young Bonapartes at Aix, they leaped at once to the conclusion that Hortense was organising an army for the invasion of France, and that the youthful Napoleon's tin sword, and Louis's little drum, would prove more prolific of mischief and slaughter than the dragon's teeth of old. Meanwhile Hortense became desirous of quitting Savoy, and of settling for a time at Constance, in the grand duchy of Baden. But to reach that city it would be necessary to traverse nearly the whole of Switzerland, and this she soon found was not to be done without express permission from the government of each of the cantons through which she would have to pass. While she was engaged in this important negotiation, the day arrived for the departure of her eldest son.

It is said there are few evils in life which might not be worse. Hortense thought so on this occasion, because the crimes perpetrated in the contiguous provinces of France, where generals Brune and La Garde had just been assassinated, made her fear for the lives of her children. One of them at least, she thought, would be in safety with her husband in

Rome, and this blunted the pangs of separation. But little Louis was incapable of deriving any relief from such philosophy. He had never before been separated for a single hour from his brother, and now threw his arms about his neck, and kissed him, and cried as if his heart would break. He is said to have been at the time a gentle, timid child, speaking little, but thinking and feeling a great deal. Sorrow for the loss of his brother—for separation at such an age seems equivalent to death—threw him into the jaundice, which however, though it weakened him considerably, by no means endangered his life. He had now practically become the only child of his mother, who thenceforward concentrated the greater part of her maternal tenderness on him.

CHAP. XI.

ADVENTURES ON THE WAY TO CONSTANCE.

At this time the health of the queen became so extremely bad, that all who took any interest in her feared for her life. She could scarcely take any nourishment, and delighted in nothing but sitting alone, in solitary places, sketching the beauties of the Alps, or reflecting moodily on the misfortunes of her family. At length, on the 28th of November, she quitted Aix, with her little son, and arrived on the evening of the same day, at her villa of Pregny, near Geneva, half dead with fatigue and cold. The authorities of the little republic once more took alarm, and in the course of the night despatched a body of cavalry, to see, in the language of old Rome, that the state received no detriment from the presence of this dangerous woman. One reason for so extraordinary a proceeding, was the belief of the council that Hortense's *femme-de-chambre*, who was as tall and robust as a man, was no other than Joseph in disguise; and, considering the tricks and arts of the

Bonaparte family, this was by no means an extravagant supposition. Their fears were of short continuance, for the queen set out immediately on her
way to Constance.

It is very certain that she constituted at this
time a centre of interest to all the wandering Bonapartists who, in disguise and poverty, were flying for
their lives. It would be endless to relate all the
anecdotes which might be collected in proof of this.

In the course of her journey, just before arriving
at the little town of Morat in the canton of Fri-
bourg, she got out of her carriage and stopped to
sketch a landscape on the way-side. The courier
had been sent ahead to order dinner at the inn,
while the other domestics were grouped in circle
round the queen. They had been but a short time
in this situation before ten or a dozen men, wrapped
in long cloaks, approached from different points, and
gradually drew round them. The queen's female
attendants became alarmed, when one of these men
approaching Hortense, inquired whether she were
not the Duchesse de St. Leu. Upon being answered
in the affirmative, he said, "Then we have orders to
arrest you and your suite, and to keep you prisoners
at the auberge, until we shall receive instructions
from the governor of the canton to release you."

Hortense of course had no choice but to submit, and proceeded to Morat in the midst of *gens d'armes*, and a multitude of peasants who had flocked together from the neighbouring fields. No evil arose from this incident save a disagreeable delay; and after passing through Berne, Frauenfield, Winterthur, and several other places, they arrived at Constance. As the grand duchy of Baden had not been enumerated among the countries in which the members of the Bonaparte family were permitted to live, it is not easy to understand why Hortense should have thought of going thither; but she had performed a weary journey, in order to reach it, and looked forward to the enjoyment of a little rest.

The first thing, of course, was to find a house, in the choice of which she was determined by a reference to the picturesque. It may be considered somewhat surprising, that a person in so much trouble should have thought of such matters; but whoever has gone through similar trials, must know that it is precisely under the pressure of great misfortunes that we most covet the repose which springs from contemplating the serene aspect of nature. The lake of Constance is so vast that it might from many points of view be mistaken for the open sea, were it not for those snowy sierras which tower beyond it into the empyrean, and mingle imperceptibly with the blue.

In order to shed a damp over all her poetical feelings, Hortense soon received a letter from her cousin, the grand duchess of Baden, containing the agreeable piece of information, that her husband, in obedience to the wishes of the allied sovereigns, must refuse her the poor satisfaction of residing within his territories. Disgusted and fatigued with persecution, she determined to take no notice of this polite insinuation, and went on looking for a residence, until she found one somewhat adapted to her taste. As this was perhaps the place in which the mind of Louis Napoleon first began to develope itself, and was brought habitually into contact with the grand aspects of nature, I shall introduce a brief description of it here.

Having searched for a considerable time, they at length found a large house, which Hortense thought would suit her. It stood on the tongue of land that approaches Constance, at the point where the bed of the waters, becoming suddenly narrower, barely affords a passage to the Rhine, which connects the upper and lower lake. Here is thrown across the stream that great old-fashioned covered bridge, which forms the entrance to the city from the duchy of Baden.

As in most other Swiss houses, all the chambers of the Duchesse of St. Leu's new dwelling opened upon a wooden gallery, extending round the building, and had no internal communication with each other. Hortense presided over the arrangement of the furniture which had been brought from Paris, and delighted herself with the idea that she once more possessed a home. Shortly afterwards, her tranquillity was again interrupted by a letter from the wife of her brother, deploring the sudden loss of a child. Eugène was at this time living at Berg, in Bavaria, and Hortense immediately set out with her son Louis to afford what consolation she could to the bereaved mother. On their arrival at Berg, young Louis Napoleon displayed some timidity at finding himself in the midst of so many strange faces, but soon got used to his cousins, male and female, and played and romped with them to their heart's content. Having remained some time at Berg, they returned to Constance, and shortly afterwards Hortense set out for the canton of Appenzell, leaving her son Louis under the care of the Abbé Bertrand and M. de Marmold.

During this trip, she had a little love adventure,

to which, perhaps, it may not be too much to devote
a few words. Soon after arriving at Geiss, she
made the acquaintance of the landamann, a widower,
with grown-up daughters; several visits were made
and returned; and the manners of Hortense, so gay,
so easy and fascinating, in spite of her ill-health,
produced a terrible effect on the susceptible Swiss.
Republican as he was, his objections to royalty at
once melted away before the brilliance of her charms;
and at length, love rendering him desperate, he made
her a formal offer of marriage. " But, my friend,"
replied Hortense, " I am married already." " That
does not at all signify," replied the landamann, "since
here in Switzerland nothing is more easy than to
obtain a divorce." But her experience of matri-
mony had not been sufficiently agreeable to induce
her to make a second trial of it, and therefore she
retreated in the best way she could out of her difficult position.

Being on the subject of love, I may as well
relate another anecdote, though lying chronologi-
cally, far removed from her journey to Appenzell.
During Hortense's unmarried days, she inspired a
young French nobleman with a furious passion for
her. Having danced with her a few times at the
Tuileries, and received, or fancied he received,

encouragement from her manner, love so completely turned his brain, that he was no longer master of himself. Whenever Mdlle. Beauharnais appeared in the streets, in the public gardens, at church, or at the opera, there this persevering lover was sure to be found. When she went abroad in a carriage, he rode alongside of it, sometimes throwing in flowers to her, sometimes locks of his hair, and occasionally, for he was a poet, verses of his own composition. Hortense seldom walked out; but when she did, this Parisian Quixote used to throw himself on his knees before her, and endeavour to express his passion, by the most extravagant words and gestures. He indulged in the same freaks at the Tuileries, no matter who might be present. At first she rather encouraged these antics; but when he followed her to the theatre, and prostrating himself on the earth before her, gave way to all sorts of wild transports, supplicating, gesticulating, laughing, crying, all at the same time, Hortense perceived that the joke had been carried too far, and to deliver herself from the young man's importunities, she caused him to be confined in a mad-house.

CHAP. XII.

ANECDOTES OF HIS BOYHOOD.

THE education of her son now formed the principal
occupation of Hortense, her fondness for him being
her ruling sentiment; and finding no suitable masters
at Constance, she herself gave him lessons in drawing, dancing, and all the other arts of pleasing.
The evening, until he went to bed, was taken up
with such reading as she thought calculated to improve his mind, and accommodated to the lessons he
had studied during the day. Sometimes it was a
book of travels connected with that portion of geo-
graphy which then occupied him, sometimes an
account of particular traits of character, illustrative
of his historical studies. The Saturday of every
week Hortense gave up entirely to him. He was
then made to repeat all he had learned during the
preceding days of the week; and though what he
had been engaged in might have been Latin, or
something else lying equally beyond her own ac-
quirements, she wished to make him feel that

nothing he did or thought of could be indifferent to
her, and that she desired above all things to see him
make progress.

But he was a difficult boy to teach; boisterous
restlessness, which the French disguise under the
name of vivacity, rendered it more troublesome to
keep him in order than to make him learn, though
both tasks were far from easy. It was to little
purpose that the good Abbé exerted all his ingenuity and zeal; master Louis frequently escaped
from him, and Hortense soon became convinced that
it would be necessary to place him in the hands of
more vigorous and authoritative teachers. Though
the Abbé Bertrand always remained in the queen's
household, he yielded up the sovereignty of the
birch to M. Lebas, a man of merit and learning,
afterwards Greek professor, in the Paris Athenæum.
The father of this man was a Republican of the
school of Robespierre, and when that great revolutionary chief was murdered, shot himself to avoid
the disgrace of surviving him.

Louis Napoleon was now beginning to exhibit an
independent character. What rendered the task
of the Abbé Bertrand more arduous, was that
quickness and readiness of mind which speedily
enabled the boy to find an answer for everything,

and induced him always to ask a reason for what he was required to do. At Constance, as at Aix, Louis was in the habit of playing with all the boys of the neighbourhood, among whom was the miller's son. The father of this lad lived on the bridge over the Rhine, close to Hortense's house, and the young miller, being older than Louis, often tempted him to go beyond the grounds, which he had been forbidden to do. One day when he had made his escape, and the Abbé at the top of his voice was shouting to him to come back, Mdlle. Cochelet, his mother's principal companion, observed him return, making a most ludicrous figure. He was in his shirt-sleeves, and walking barefoot carelessly through the mud and snow. Had he been able to reach his own room unobserved, it would have been all very well, but he was put considerably out of countenance by being found in such a pickle in the street. Upon being questioned how he came to be in that condition, he explained, that while playing at the entrance to the garden, he had seen a family go by, so poor, and so miserable, that it was quite painful to look at them. He therefore took off his shoes, and put them on the feet of one of the children, and gave his coat to another, because, as he said, he happened to have no money to give them.

They who best knew him, during his boyhood and his youth, have observed that many similar traits of liberality might be related of him. Hortense, who was herself full of generosity, experienced peculiar delight in perceiving him perform acts of this kind, but objected strongly to having any notice taken of them in the presence of her son, fearing lest he should be tempted to do, from vanity, what she wished to proceed from the natural impulses of his heart.

As Louis Napoleon grew up, his features, which had been delicate in childhood, became less regular than expressive, or, in other words, degenerated into plainness, if not into ugliness. Yet he always retained during his boyhood a certain mildness in his looks, together with much intelligence and sentiment, which rendered him extremely interesting. This expression, according to his friends, sprang from the sensibility of his heart, and was afterwards united with that calm energy which constitutes the basis of his character. There is no doubt that many Italian ladies who lived at the court of Alexander the Sixth made similar remarks on the youthful Cæsar Borgia; and we know, from history, that Claudius Domitius Nero displayed in his earlier years so much sentiment and sensibility that, had he died then, he might through all future ages have disputed with the son of Vespasian the reputation of being the delight of mankind. Possibly, had Louis Napoleon succeeded regularly to the throne of France, he might never have committed those crimes which now shed so dark a stain over his history, and would have appeared to deserve the praises bestowed on him in his early years, when he really was generous, enthusiastic, and full of sympathy for others. To some extent he may have owed the development of those qualities to the education he received from his mother; grave, simple, and invigorating. This could hardly fail to produce excellent results on a nature which panegyrists have called so privileged. But these writers are so carried away by their prejudices for the Bonaparte family that their testimony is of little value.

In the beginning of 1817, Hortense received an invitation from her brother, which was seconded by one from King Maximilian, to take up her residence in Bavaria, and prepared with regret to quit Constance, because she had there made for herself many friends. Such, however, was the fascination of her character, that she could easily do the same anywhere. She seems to have possessed extraordinary conversational powers, and her alliance with the

Bonaparte family imparted to these, in the estimation of most persons, a charm, the origin of which they could not perceive, and would have been slow to acknowledge if they could. But the vulgar everywhere love to associate with persons who are or have been of consequence, and easily discover in them agreeable qualities, which their position only renders visible.

To prevent disappointment on her arrival at Augsburg, she despatched her steward, M. de Marmold, with money to purchase for her a house, as she disliked living in a hired one. But the aspect of German cities is at best little calculated to inspire Frenchmen with agreeable ideas. Their heavy sombre architecture, the melancholy of the climate, which resembles that of England, and the slow plodding superstitious character of the people, which corresponds exactly with the nature of their country, —all these things combine to overshadow and depress the mind of persons accustomed to livelier society and a brighter sky. No wonder, therefore, that M. de Marmold returned to Constance from his Bavarian expedition grievously oppressed with sadness.

While describing the circumstances under which Hortense and her children left Paris, I observed that she found herself under the necessity of selling a number of pictures to defray the expenses of her journey. That fact, if regarded by itself, might suggest very false ideas. Though pressed at the moment for a certain amount of money, we must by no means imagine her to have been poor. On the contrary, like every other member of the Bonaparte family, she had taken ample care to provide for the future, knowing the effect of opulence on nearly all mankind. Wherever she went she found it practicable to attach numerous persons to the fortunes of her family by strong ties of interest, to purchase houses and lands, to surround herself with agreeable natural objects, to enlarge and beautify her dwellings, and to lay out her grounds with taste. By degrees, moreover, her household came to be composed of persons who understood her views, and carefully studied to fulfil them.

Her favourite acquisition was an estate in the canton of Thurgovia, where she built the château of Arenenberg, to which her name and that of her son will give a celebrity in history. Thither she intended to return every autumn, partly in order to enjoy the picturesque aspect of the Alps, and partly that she might preserve her hold on the minds of the Swiss people, by accustoming them to her presence, and to the advantages which her residence procured to the neighbourhood.

CHAP. XIII.

THE COLLEGE OF AUGSBURG.

THE situation of the château of Arenenberg was in the highest degree striking and picturesque. Standing midway on the slope of a wooded hill, it commanded an extensive prospect over the lake of Constance, with its richly fringed shores, and fairy islands. Whoever has lived in Switzerland must have become deeply conscious of the effect produced by its wild and savage grandeur upon the mind, which it at once hushes into repose, and penetrates with profound emotions. It is very certain that external nature, in those regions, blends itself more intimately than in the north with our inner life. Alps, avalanches, snow storms, frozen seas, forests of dark pine, precipices, cataracts, unfathomable gulfs in which immense rivers appear to lose themselves, as they plunge down out of sight between dizzy rocks, —all these things speak to the imagination, and arm it, so to say, with energy to struggle against any possible combination of organised beings.

Hortense might almost be said, at this time, to have ceased altogether to exist on her own account, and to live only for her younger son, whom she looked upon as the hope of her heart and house. Having made all necessary arrangements, she quitted Constance on the 6th of May, 1817. Their principal object for removing to Augsburg was the existence in that city of an excellent college, where she hoped her son Louis might obtain that instruction which neither the Abbé Bertrand nor M. de Lebas was able to supply.

She was in all likelihood swayed by the opinion then beginning to be current in Europe, that the Germans are great masters of the art of education. That the knowledge of their professors is sometimes extensive, it would be unjust to deny. They are often distinguished for their familiarity with the learned languages of antiquity, and for whatever else we comprehend under the name of masculine accomplishments. But it may perhaps be doubted whether the Germans at all understand the art of education in the old Hellenic sense, in which it signified, not the mere act of imparting information, but the disciplining and training of the mind so as to give it strength, flexibility, and courage. Up to this hour the Germans, as a people, are deficient in these qualities. They are ingenious, erudite, laborious, but mistake the love of strange paradoxes for boldness of intellect, and substitute the pleasures of a vague and shadowy world, created by the imagination, for philosophical wisdom and the enjoyment of civil liberty.

Whatever may be the value of the things taught in Germany, Louis Napoleon assiduously applied himself to the study of them. During four years while the college was open, and the lectures were going forward, he remained at Augsburg; but with the commencement of the vacations, his mother hastened to leave Germany, and took him along with her to Switzerland or Italy. It was at these times that he received what I call his education. No writer, so far as I am aware, has described the process pursued by Hortense in the development of her son's faculties. There was probably very little system in it, and in fact it may have consisted altogether in that vivifying influence which one mind, suggestive, plastic and powerful, produces upon another. She contained within herself the traditions of the Revolution, of the Consulate, of the Empire, and the germs of numerous virtues and qualities which circumstances had never perhaps fully ripened. To a thoughtful, ambitious boy, the

instructions of such a woman were of infinitely
greater value than the eloquence of a thousand
professors.   She poured ideas into his soul from her
own kindred spirit, and illustrated every great lesson
she gave by the force of her own example.

It is not to be doubted that Louis Napoleon's
education in Switzerland exerted a considerable influence over his thoughts.   It invited him to medi-
tate, to plan, to organise political conspiracies for the
purpose of reconstructing the fortunes of his family.
With all the appearance of bold thinkers, the French
have still preserved much of the chivalrous servility
of the middle ages.   Give them a great name, and
they intrigue for it, struggle for it, conspire for it,
fight for it, die for it.   It never occurs to them that
their own enthusiasm creates the idol they so de-
voutly worship.   In England, the career of Louis
Napoleon would have been simply impossible.   He
might have lived and died among us, without acquiring a reputation for anything.   As a writer, he
is scarcely above mediocrity, and he has no talents
of any other kind which would have raised him to
eminence here.   When we had a pretender who
really was full of chivalry, he could make nothing of
us, and we could make nothing of him.   There is no
sympathy for knight errantry in the English charac-

ter. But no sooner were the French made sensible
that a young man, who might be nursed up into a
pretender, lived a little way beyond the frontier,
than they got up an interest in him, and the way to
the château of Arenenberg soon became as well
known as that to the parish church.

And now Hortense's hoarded treasures, laid out
with judgment in hospitality, gradually excited admiration, and created partisans. The Bonaparte
family and its connections dotted the map of
Europe. They were to be found everywhere, from
the moors of Scotland to the marches of Ancona,
and their mutual visits, their correspondence, their
political and scientific activity, enabled them to exert immense influence in times pre-eminently un-
settled. The education of Louis Napoleon in
Switzerland so closely resembled that of the young
engineer officers, that no particular account of it
need to be given. What imparted to it a peculiar
character was this, that while the other students,
through the narrowness of their means, were compelled to spend their vacations at their own homes
among the mountains, Louis Napoleon went frequently with his mother to Bavaria, to Tuscany, to
Rome, where he enjoyed the further advantage of
constantly listening to the conversation of persons

who had seen the world, acquired some knowledge
of statesmanship, and in many cases played no in-
considerable part in the great drama of nations,
which opened up the nineteenth century.

The Swiss system of education is so well calculated
to develope those faculties of the mind which may
be termed practical, that it is surprising it does not
bring forth into notice more remarkable men.   It
must, however, be admitted to have done much.
Throughout both hemispheres, in the United States,
in Italy, Germany, France, Russia, Turkey, and
among the Mahrattas of Hindústan, Swiss officers
have raised themselves to high command, and acquired ample fortunes.

The system of training which led to such results,
deserves to be studied and described at greater length
than would be proper in a work like the present.
It has something of a Spartan character.   The
young men, after having gone through their studies
in the college, are taken out to contemplate, from a
military point of view, the whole aspect of the
country.   They traverse wild gorges, they climb
mountains, they bivouac at the foot of glaciers, and
are expected to triangulate, with more or less
exactitude, the whole area of the canton in which
they are educated.   This process at once strengthens

their bodies and their minds, accustoms them to the
changes and inclemency of the weather, and to provide for their own comforts in the midst of disad-
vantageous circumstances.   Milton long ago re-
commended, with all his stately eloquence, a similar
plan for the training of youth, in conjunction with
a much greater amount of learning than falls to the
lot of Swiss mathematicians or engineers.

Louis Napoleon's work, entitled "Political and
Military Considerations on Switzerland," may be
regarded as one of the fruits of the studies he pursued at Thun.   It is the result of much thought,
reading, and experience.   Having by observation
become familiar with most of the cantons, topogra-
phically and strategically, he was enabled to reason,
in an acute and striking manner, on the resources
and wants of the country.   No doubt his views are
everywhere those of a Frenchman of the Napoleonic
school.   The idea of centralisation dominates and
subdues everything, and betrays him into criticisms
on the Swiss policy and government, which, though
ingenious in themselves, are irreconcileable with the
facts of history.   In some respects the Swiss system is
like our own, irregular, heterogeneous, and incapable
of explanation by the ordinary laws of society ; that
is, the theory upon which their civil polity is based

is too subtle, too profound, too remote from ordinary
analogies, to be grasped by ordinary investigation.
It may be inferred, however, from its admirable
working in practice, that it is founded on the principles of human nature.

But at the period in which these considerations were
written, Louis Napoleon was a Republican, though
he experienced the utmost difficulty in reconciling
his political ideas with the traditions of his family ;
above all, with his respect for Napoleon. Among
his chief mental idiosyncracies derived from the
same source, were his hatred of England, and the
resolution, then cherished by nearly all Frenchmen,
to avenge the battle of Waterloo. His philosophy
had not yet taught him to look with calmness on the
events of history, and to reflect that all nations which
make a great figure in the world must necessarily
alternate victories with reverses. England, in its
opposition to France, was actuated, first, by the
principle of self-preservation, then by the desire to
preserve the balance of power on the continent, and
afterwards, perhaps, by grand schemes of ambition.
But with the events of those times, the feelings to
which they gave birth should be allowed to pass
away. In the estimation of philosophy, it would be
as rational for the people of this country to think of

avenging the battle of Hastings, as for the French to
aim perpetually at vindicating upon England the
battle of Waterloo.   Both events have passed into
the domain of history, and stand there recorded for
the instruction of posterity.   The men of the present
day neither won nor lost them, and sufficient to each
age are the passions and disasters thereof.   The
feeling of vengeance is incompatible with civilisation,
and Frenchmen might as well goad themselves incessantly with the remembrance of Cressy, Poictiers,
and Agincourt, as with that of the combat on the
plains of Belgium.

The "Considerations," however, upon the whole, are
both curious and instructive.   The author evidently,
when he wrote, was actuated by strong convictions
in favour of freedom, for it cannot be said that he
was ever impassioned or enthusiastic.   He contended
for the absolute liberty of the press, and exhibited
some warmth, when, to use his own language, he
came to make use of the great word Republic.   But
in many parts he loses sight of the object he pro-
fesses to have in view, and sinks into the advocate of
a perpetual alliance with France.   In the course of
two or three years, he himself narrowly escaped
becoming the cause of a destructive war between
France and Switzerland.

PART THE SECOND.

~~~~~

CHAPTER I.

THE BONAPARTES BEYOND THE ALPS.

I HAVE now arrived at what may be called the
Italian episode in the life of Louis Napoleon. He
was then in principle a Republican, thinking more of
the good of others than of his own advancement; at
least, this constituted at the time, his political profession of faith. He had long been in the habit of
going every year with his mother to pass the winter
in Italy. Nearly all the members of the Bonaparte
family were scattered over the peninsula; in Tuscany,
or the Roman States; and possessed palaces at Ancona, at Florence, and in the Eternal City. His
brother Napoleon had married one of his cousins,
a daughter of Joseph, formerly King of Spain, and
resided with her at Florence, apparently in the same
palace with his father Louis.

The family was thus situated when the revolution

of July took place. I was myself in France at the time, and enjoyed many opportunities of becoming acquainted with the real feelings of the people. According to some writers, the Napoleonist party had its roots everywhere in the people, in the administration, in the army, and even in the peerage. But if so, these roots were very carefully concealed. No cry was raised in favour of the empire; the word indeed was scarcely pronounced, except by General Gourgaud, a weak and fanatical soldier, whose voice, when he ventured to raise it in Paris, was immediately silenced by fierce and indignant murmurs.

No doubt there still lingered among the peasants and the lower orders generally, a partiality for Napoleon; but the more respectable classes were divided into two parties, of which the one was Republican, and the other Bourbonist.

Secretly in the capital, the Duke of Orleans had long been laying out his immense fortune in purchasing himself friends, and organising that political movement which afterwards placed him on the throne. He had deluded many Republicans through the agency of Lafayette, a man of honest intentions and a certain influence, but weak and credulous from the beginning, and now in his old age weaker and more credulous than ever.

Paris, containing the choicest intellects in the country, was at this time filled with enthusiastic Republicans, while the departments, more especially those in the north, were eager to overthrow Charles X., and establish a democracy. Everywhere the effervescence of the young mind was extraordinary, and yet not a single voice was anywhere heard in favour of any member of the Bonaparte family. It might possibly have proved different, had one of them been on the spot to excite, by his presence, the adherents of the imperial *régime.* But the changes of government in France resemble the shifting of scenes at the theatre, rather than great political catastrophes. No time was left either to Louis Napoleon or his brother for putting forward their pretensions, and besides, the young King of Rome was still living at Vienna. The sons of Hortense were both of them energetic, and the elder, wanting employment for his mind, had conceived the idea of joining the Greek cause. He was prevented by the representations of his mother, who, appealing to his republican opinions, suggested to him that the name he bore might give a wrong character to the struggle.

In the month of November, 1830, Hortense quitted Florence for Rome, taking her son Louis along with her. What the designs of the family

really were at this time, it is now impossible to determine; but from many circumstances which they
themselves had suffered to transpire, it seems perfectly
clear that they were all, male and female, deeply engaged in fomenting the troubles of Italy. There are
persons still living who could throw light on this
subject if their own political prospects would permit
them; but as this is not the case, we must be content
to infer, from facts and events, the nature and
purpose of their secret machinations.

The whole country, from the Alps to the Faro of
Messina, was in a state of great excitement, and all
those societies which had for years been labouring
to bring about a revolution, now hoped the time
was at length come to accomplish their great purpose.
The effervescence of the public mind was perhaps
greatest in Romagna, where the desire for political
emancipation penetrated through every rank of society. Travellers arriving from beyond the Alps
were stopped in the streets of Rome, and conjured
by the populace to describe the new revolution
which had taken place in France.

Unfortunately for the Italians, a prince, the Duke of
Modena, had been admitted into the secret of their designs, which he hoped so to fashion and direct as to lead
to his being proclaimed King of all Italy. For this

purpose, and for this alone, he entered into the general conspiracy, and consented to foment those troubles the elements of which had long existed throughout the country. But the chief conspirators were inimical to all forms of royalty; what they aimed at was independence first, and then liberty. Perhaps their ideas were not very clear, or their opinions very decided; but they would appear to have, in most cases, ventured to dream of the reconstruction of the Roman Commonwealth.

The young men of the Bonaparte family, having long made profession of republicanism, were initiated in all those mysteries which had been organised for the regeneration of Italy, and it may not perhaps be too much to say that the elder members of the family, including even Cardinal Fesch and Louis, ex-king of Holland, were conscious of the intentions of their younger kinsmen, and ready to co-operate for their fulfilment. They had preserved from the ruins of the empire very considerable sums of money, though not so much perhaps as popular rumour attributes to them, and it seems probable that they made use of their opulence for the furtherance of certain political schemes, which, it is hardly to be doubted, they had formed in Italy. Louis Philippe had stolen a march upon them in France, and they seemed, by the course of events, to have been irrevocably excluded from that kingdom.

But the misgovernment which unquestionably
existed in Naples, in the Papal States, in the Lom-
bardo-Venetian kingdom, in Piedmont, and even
Tuscany, encouraged them to hope that they might
erect for themselves an empire beyond the Alps
equal in power, and far superior in interest and
beauty. Secret councils were therefore held by the
whole family at Rome, and couriers, agents, and
emissaries were despatched in all directions, to
hasten the decisions of their friends and bring affairs
to a crisis. I am far from censuring these movements. There is no government of Italy, if we
except that of Piedmont, which it would not still
be an act of humanity to overthrow, and at the time
of which I speak, even that government formed no ex-
ception.* I therefore consider the conduct of the Bonaparte family not only justifiable, but praiseworthy,
even though they should have had the intention of putting themselves in the places of the sovereigns they
dethroned. It was impossible they should prove
worse than their predecessors, and it was extremely
probable that they would prove much better.

I do not lay much stress on the republican posses-

---

* Louis Napoleon himself, while enlarging on the achievements of his uncle Joseph, speaks of Italy as "un pays avili par
le déspotisme le plus brutal." (ii. 421.)

sions of Louis Napoleon and his brother. If they were sincere, which is of course possible, they would in all likelihood have taken advantage of circumstances to raise themselves on the ruins of the Republic; the younger certainly would. However, the point on which I desire to insist at present is, that Louis Napoleon, in 1830 and 1831, was a conspirator, and attempted to subvert the established governments of Italy for the professed purpose of founding a Republic.

In the course of the winter the disorders of Rome increased, and the Papal government apprehended more and more danger from the presence and intrigues of the Bonaparte family. To what extent Louis Napoleon was involved in the proceedings of the Carbonari is not exactly known; but it is certain that he excited the populace by appearing in the streets on horseback, with the *tricolore*, the symbol of the French Republic, ostentatiously displayed about him. Any person less powerfully supported would have been arrested, and thrown into a dungeon; but he had an uncle in the conclave, and the vigorous old Cardinal, partial to revolutionary movements, upheld for a while the interests of his nephew. But at length the Pope became irritated, and sent an officer with a troop of horse to seize him in his lodgings and conduct him to the frontier.

I have observed repeatedly upon the opulence possessed by all the elder members of the Bonaparte family. No account is of course to be made of popular exaggeration, which attributed millions without end to Madame Mère. Her brother also, Cardinal Fesch, having enjoyed numerous opportunities of scraping wealth together, had diligently made use of them, for the purpose, perhaps, of laying out his hoards on a fitting occasion in the purchase of power. But in proportion as his treasures grew, his fondness for them grew also, and many an amusing anecdote is told of the difficulties encountered by those who sought to awaken his slumbering liberality.

Jerome, once at Madame Campan's *pension*, greatly amused his sister Caroline and Hortense Beauharnais with an extremely droll illustration of his uncle's besetting sin. By the way also, it must be acknowledged that the young scapegrace's narrative reflected more credit on his wit than on his principles. Napoleon, it is well known, was far from niggardly in the allowances he made from the public purse to his relatives, and Jerome, though then a young man, enjoyed a handsome revenue. Being fond of pleasure, however, he often found means in Paris to arrive at the bottom of his purse.

He usually in such predicaments had recourse to General Murat; but this generous friend being absent, he was once reduced to his wits' end, for want of twenty-five louis. After meditating for some time, he thought of his uncle Fesch, and proceeded in high expectation to his eminence's palace.

It was a grand reception day, and numerous princes and grandees, spiritual and temporal, were assembled at dinner. Jerome was invited to join them, and did so, nothing lothe. On rising from table, the guests proceeded into that splendid gallery in which the Cardinal had brought together some of the finest masterpieces of painting. Jerome now took his uncle into the embrasure of a window, and laid his case before him. Twenty-five louis! The Cardinal's sacerdotal blood ran chill at the bare mention of such a sum. He flatly refused his nephew's request. Upon this, Jerome, whose companions perhaps were at that moment impatiently expecting him at the gaming-table, became angry, and raising his glance to a magnificent portrait by Vandyke, which hung exactly opposite on the wall, he drew his sword, and exclaimed, "Look at that old rascal! He is laughing at my disappointment; —I will go and poke his eyes out!" To preserve a picture, probably worth more than a thousand pounds, uncle Fesch drew forth his purse, and doled out grudgingly to Jerome the sum he requested.

As it was evident that a conspiracy existed, and must soon result in an insurrection, Hortense, whatever may have been her ambition, was not sorry to behold her son removed from the dangers of the first outbreak. Indeed, she probably thought it desirable that he should remain at a distance, till the rough work had been done by others, after which he might make his appearance, and gather the golden fruits of the insurrection. The populace became more disturbed, the government more alarmed, and the aspect of events more dark and threatening. It seemed clear that a popular rising was close at hand, and she dreaded the repetition in the Eternal City of those fearful scenes which, at the close of the last century, had converted Paris into a slaughter-house.

Men from the Sabine mountains, from the marshes, from the quarries, and from all other parts of Italy, began to show their fierce aspect in the streets of Rome. Knots of conspirators met in the public places. There was an inexplicable movement in the lower classes of the multitude. The *cafés* were filled with swarthy strangers, and a population, remarkable for its careless gaiety, became at once serious and reflective. The sacerdotal government, even with the Jesuits at its command, was completely nonplussed. Everybody felt that events of terrible import were on the eve of their accomplishment, but no one knew how or where the tempest would burst.

CHAP. II.

LOUIS NAPOLEON ENGAGES IN THE INSURRECTION IN
ROMAGNA.

IN this state of things Hortense thought it advisable
to make her escape to Florence, where she hoped to
be able to retain her sons till the propitious moment.
On arriving, however, at the Tuscan capital she
found they had set out for the Roman States, where
most of the provinces from the Tyrrhene Sea to the
Adriatic were now in a state of open revolt. Whatever may have been her ambition, she could not in
such a situation fail to experience much anxiety and
alarm. Louis Napoleon had left a letter for her
containing the reasons by which he and his brother
had been actuated. He made it perfectly clear that
he had long formed a part of the conspiracy, and
before he left Rome had advanced much too far to
recede. " Your affection," he said to his mother,
" will enable you to understand us. We have
entered into engagements and must keep them;
and the name we bear compels us to aid those
unhappy populations which invite us to assist them.

Set me right in the eyes of my sister-in-law, who no doubt blames me for having led away her husband, who is much grieved he should ever have been under the necessity of concealing from her, one single action of his life."

When Hortense had read this letter, she felt all the agonies their rashness was calculated to inspire, and spent the whole night in writing to them such instructions as she thought suited to the moment. Her eldest son's wife, then with child, was in extreme grief at the desertion of her husband, and the father of the young men, weak and querulous, overwhelmed Hortense with his fears and apprehensions. With a feebleness altogether unmanly, he went to and fro bewailing himself, but refused to do anything for the preservation of his sons. All his efforts were exhausted, and he endeavoured to prevail on their mother to return to the scene of civil war, and perform his duties for him.

At first Louis Napoleon and his brother were raised to the principal commands in the insurgent army, but their youth and inexperience rendered it impossible for them to retain their posts, which were transferred to Generals Sercognani and Armandi. Nevertheless they had done much towards strengthening the cause of the insurrection. They had

organised defensive operations from Foligno to
Civita Castellana. The youth both of city and
country obeyed them; though imperfectly armed
they sought to avail themselves of all the resources
which the country afforded, and were preparing to
take Civita Castellana and liberate the political
prisoners who had been for eight years confined
in its dungeons.

Could they succeed in this enterprise, there
would be nothing to obstruct their march to Rome.
The father of the young men, who, during the
previous part of his life, had treated them with
neglect, appeared to be now inspired with extraordinary solicitude. But it moved him to no
extraordinary exertion on his own part. All his
energies were confined to tormenting their mother,
and urging her to go after them into the disturbed
districts, and bring them back to Florence. He
left her not one moment's rest, but constantly
renewed his entreaties. Hortense, on the other
hand, contended it was beyond her power to induce
them to relinquish the enterprise; she could only
engage to restore them to their family, if they
themselves wished to return. But should they have
taken any active part, she could not even endeavour
to persuade them to desert their friends. Besides,

her going would be viewed with great suspicion, and she would be supposed to be carrying them millions to enable the insurgents to continue the war. In this case she would herself be compromised, and there would be no one left who could be useful to them.

If we can entirely trust the representations of Hortense, her husband was at this time quite beside himself. Her reasoning produced no conviction on his mind, and his excitement was so great that he even went to the Austrian ambassador, to entreat what was impossible, namely, that he should demand his children from the advanced posts of the army. To account for the weakness, mental and bodily, of this poor prince, Napoleon, one morning at Verona, related during breakfast a very curious story. " Here in this very city," he said, " a circumstance occurred in one of our early campaigns, which produced the most disastrous effect on poor Louis' health and understanding. About one o'clock in the morning a woman of whom he knew scarcely anything broke into the house; and ever since that time he has been subject to nervous agitations, more or less violent according to the changes of the atmosphere, but of which no art can cure him."

In some respects to calm her husband's mind, Hortense consented to proceed to the Tuscan frontiers, and from thence to write to her sons, requiring them to return immediately. From this point her history becomes the same with theirs. She expected no result from what she undertook, but went merely to please their father.

When she applied for her passports the Prince Corsini, brother of the Tuscan minister, called upon her. His object, no doubt, was to discover her real sentiments, and also, if possible, how far she was implicated in the proceedings of her sons. She explained that her only object in going to the frontier was to satisfy her husband's wishes. The prince then proposed a plan by which means he said she might bring her sons back. This plan, it must be owned, was highly complimentary to the affections of those sons, but not so perhaps to their patriotism or to her affection for them. It was this: that she should proceed to the frontier and thence write to them to say she was ill, upon which the prince did not doubt they would come to her. If they did, a troop of Tuscan horse was to be placed in ambush, who would immediately seize them and bring them back by force to the capital. Hortense, however, refused to put this stratagem in practice, preferring that they should take the chances of war than that she should be a party to laying such a snare for them.

It is certain that the whole Napoleon family was at this time in a state of much excitement. One of the sons of Lucien escaped from his father's château, with the obvious intention of joining the insurgents. But his mother remembering the obligations of the family to the Pope, who had in fact created the principalities of Canino and Musignano for Lucien and his eldest son, caused the young man to be waylaid, arrested and thrown into prison. This was the example they wished Hortense to follow, but, as might have been foreseen, without effect.

It is difficult for any one but a mother to comprehend the excitement and apprehensions of Hortense at this moment; she walked her room all night forming schemes for recovering her sons, and flying with them she knew not whither. At length she determined to take refuge with them in Turkey, which had been described to her in glowing colours by the Duke de Rovigo.

Meanwhile their father Louis acted like a madman. He caused their mother to write to General Armanai, who held the chief command among the insurgents, and who had been their eldest son's tutor, requesting him to dismiss them. He refused to send them their horses or any assistance in money, and thus at once

neutralise their chances of being useful, and of
escaping with their lives, in case of reverses. To
some extent therefore he may be accused as one of
the causes of what happened. The young men had
set out with little beyond their courage and their
enthusiasm, and their mother now thought she beheld
them abandoned to their own resources in the midst
of difficulties and dangers.

Louis Napoleon and his brother were in the meantime beset with still greater inquietudes. Nothing
succeeded according to their expectations. The
greatest consternation prevailed at Rome. People
exclaimed on all sides, that their name was the
signal for invasion, and diplomacy in fact made it
the pretext of that intervention which had previously
been decided upon. The letter of an ambassador,
which fell into their mother's hands, spoke of her
sons in the following terms:

"These young men, who still fancy themselves
imperial princes, if taken prisoners, will soon find
what they really are, by the manner in which we
shall treat them."

No stress can be laid on the public acts and
letters of the Bonaparte family at this period. To
cover their real designs, it may have been agreed
beween them beforehand, that while the young

men incited and led the revolt, their older and more
influential relatives should appear to condemn their
proceedings. Had success attended their efforts it
would have been easy to explain everything. But in
case of failure, the non-participation of the elders
would still maintain the position of the family, and
preserve resources for the future. At any rate
there is much confusion in all the accounts I have
seen of these transactions. As far as possible, I have
endeavoured to render my own narrative clear and
intelligible.

A provisional government had been established at
Bologna, and to its members, Cardinal Fesch, and
King Jerome who remained at Rome, wrote in conjunction with Louis to say that the young Bonapartes
were injurious to their cause, and requesting General
Armandi to remove them from the army and send
them back. They likewise wrote to the young men
themselves, at once commanding and entreating
them to return. In one word, friends, enemies,
family, everybody united their efforts to neutralise
their exertions; while the greatest enthusiasm pervaded all those parts of the country which they held;
and the brothers, measuring their success by their
own ardour and courage, already saw themselves in
hope masters of Rome, which they knew to be

in extreme consternation, and to possess very poor means of defence. In less than two days they did not doubt that the Pope would be in the hands of their small army.

It is very clear that the presence of the young Napoleon was looked upon by the Papal government as the chief strength of the insurrection. Jerome saw the Pope, a consultation was held, and an officer, M. de Stœlting, was despatched to the republican camp, authorised by His Holiness to enter into a parley with the insurgents, to inquire what they wanted, and promise compliance with their wishes. Stœlting saw the elder Napoleon, and desired him to draw up a statement of the demands and complaints of the army. He consulted its chiefs, and with their authority, delivered to the Pope's envoy a summary of the reforms for which the people asked.

Whatever may have been their secret intentions, it seems probable, that the pertinacious interference of the effete and timid members of the family at length produced its effect. The provisional government of Bologna was seized with timidity, and refused to attempt the storming of Rome. It then dispatched General Sercognani with fresh troops, to replace the young Napoleons, who left, and repaired to Ancona and afterwards to Bologna, where they offered to serve as mere volunteers.

Their father now imagined he had succeeded; but irritated by the persecution to which they had been exposed from him and the rest of the family, they wrote to say, that if they were any further interfered with, they would go and serve in the Polish insurrection, and thus place themselves beyond the reach of family intrigues. But Louis did not the less persist in his idea that Hortense ought to go after them. It soon became evident, however, that they who had removed them from their command in the army had performed for them a most dangerous service, because the government fearing them no longer, became more severe.

The Tuscan authorities now informed their father, that they should not again be suffered to reside in the grand duchy, and the Austrian ambassador added that they should henceforward be excluded from Switzerland. Jerome wrote from Rome to apprise their mother, that if taken by the Austrian army, they must be lost; and it is extremely probable that they would in fact have been immediately put to death.

The news soon reached Florence that the enemy had entered Romagna, that the roar of artillery had been heard, and no doubt was entertained of the terrible result. Everybody perceived that the cause of the insurgents was hopeless. There happened at that time to be an English gentleman at Florence whose family Hortense had formerly obliged. She sent for him now, and said he would more than save her life if he could procure for her son an English passport, representing her as an English lady travelling with her two sons through France to London. The Englishman immediately did what she required, and armed with this document, she prepared to set out in search of her sons. Her husband was so weak and timid, that she could not venture to confide her designs to him. His plan was for them to embark at Ancona for Corfu, whence they might repair to Malta, or remain somewhere under the protection of England. Hortense allowed him to suppose that she intended to do as he desired, because she knew that had the secret been confided to him, he would have betrayed it through mere imbecility. As it was, he no doubt whispered the secret of their embarkation at Ancona, which, being fully credited, threw off suspicion from her real plan.

In fact, she obtained from the Tuscan government a passport authorising her to proceed to the Roman

States, in furtherance of her ostensible design, while, as I have said, she secretly procured from her English friend another passport, with all the necessary signatures, which she concealed about her person. Her husband had lent her his travelling carriage; but the difficulty was how to escape from Florence without betraying her purpose at the first step. It was necessary she should have both her passports signed, and to bring this about she must have recourse to stratagem. She therefore went out in the evening, and driving to a particular gate, produced her English passport, and with beating heart sat in the carriage while it was examined by the police. The officer on duty came to the carriage door, and remarked that she was not leaving the city by the proper gate. She replied, "True; but I am first going to spend a few days at a villa before I proceed on my return to England." Not suspecting anything, he wished her a pleasant journey and dismissed her.

She then drove out about a half a league, with the intention of returning to the city by a different entrance. Unluckily there was no cross road, so she felt herself under the necessity of risking a discovery by coming back to the gate by which she had come out. She approached the spot where

the police were at that moment engaged with a
diligence, and then dashing along the small road at
the foot of the walls, reached another gate, through
which she went in. The police asked her where
she had been. She replied, " Out for a drive."
" What," they exclaimed, " in that travelling carriage!" "Oh," she replied, " it is one that I am about
to buy, and I am trying it." They allowed her to pass
and she returned to her hotel. The English passport
had been signed, and she could now start in the
morning with that of Tuscany. This fact I relate
to show at once the courage of the mother and the
fears of the Tuscan government which surrounds itself with such a system of passports and police. At
a reasonable hour next day she set out for Foligno,
where she determined to wait the result of the
Austrian invasion.

CHAP. III.

HIS DISCOMFITURE AND FLIGHT.

HORTENSE arrived at Perusia, the inhabitants of
which, intoxicated with a single draught of liberty as
with opium, had given themselves up to pleasure and
rejoicing.   Covered with cockades and ribands, they
appeared to be celebrating some great festival, and
seemed to imagine in their simplicity that because
they had done no harm to any one, no one would do
any harm to them.   Here, from a gentleman in the
interest of her family, she obtained all the information she needed respecting the cross-roads, places of
concealment, the state of the country, and the movements of the enemy.   Count Pepoli having come to
Perusia in search of ammunition for the insurgent
army, called upon her, and discussed the chances of
the insurrection.   Their hopes appeared to be entirely founded on the belief that there would be no
intervention; that France would keep back the
Austrians, and leave them to deal as they could with
the Pope.   But if a foreign army should appear,
all would be over, since the recruits had neither

common nor small arms, and were, in fact, altogether unprepared.

Pursuing her journey, Hortense arrived at Foligno, where she had an interview with General Sercognani, who described his distress and the courage of his young volunteers, which he was compelled to restrain because he did not possess the means of undertaking the siege of the smallest towns. "Were the Pope's soldiers," he said, "to make a sortie, the patriots would immediately rush upon them, and capture their cannon; but foreseeing this result, the enemy keep completely within their walls."

Hortense, having often conversed with able generals in France, was competent to understand and discuss the details of a campaign, and suggested to Sercognani ‚the prudence of opening a communication with the Mediterranean, so that they might be able to effect a retreat, supposing the Austrians should gain the upper hand. It appears evident that from this time no hope of victory was really entertained by the insurgents, whose best friends looked forward to nothing beyond the safety of the persons engaged.

Sercognani having occasion to despatch a courier to Ancona, Hortense sent by the same messenger a letter to her sons, impressing upon their minds the duty of taking care of themselves. She desired them to inform her, at all events, what route they designed to take, especially in case of defeat, and said she would remain where she was to receive them. Her sons now saw, and ought to have seen from the first, that nothing could be done, because the leaders of the insurrection desired to remain friends with everybody. " Woe to them," she exclaims with great justice, " who commence a revolution without possessing the means of ensuring success, or at least of rendering it probable ! "

At a later period, her younger son no doubt thought of his mother's opinion, and determined not to fail through too great moderation. Considering things from this point of view, he was perfectly right. The most rose-coloured revolutionist that ever drew sword for liberty is hated by tyrants as much as the most ferocious. Whoever rises against them, therefore, should throw moderation to the winds, and strike immediately at the root of their power. For want of being swayed by this conviction, the Italians have generally failed in their insurrections. Whenever they make up their minds in earnest to be free, they must begin by striking at the root of the evil. If they fail afterwards, they can but die, and the same fate is certain to await them even for playing harmlessly at revolution, as the unhappy Romans did in 1831.

Napoleon, the elder brother of Louis, seems to have been quite of this opinion, but to have wanted power to carry out his views. With a body of about two hundred men, he repulsed a considerably larger force of Papal troops, mingled with brigands, who emerged from the Bagne to capture the towns of Terni and Spoleto. With these ferocious enemies, Napoleon and his little band carried on a hand-to-hand contest in a wood. There was no generalship, but a great deal of courage. The leader fought like his men, and hazarded his cause that he might indulge the instinct of valour. In all wars you might find hundreds of examples of personal prowess in the most extraordinary situations, but it is only now and then in the course of many centuries, that a man appears who can think calmly in the midst of balls, pikes, and flashing sabres. Young Napoleon was successful, and led back his prisoners to Terni amidst the acclamations of the people.

While this was going forward, Louis Napoleon with another detachment of the army was hovering about the skirts of Civita Castellana, which he was preparing to assault, the Papal garrison not having taken the necessary precautions for its defence.

During these operations before the city, an officer who had remained faithful to the Pope, viewing from the walls the dispositions made by Louis Napoleon, turned round and remarked to those about him: " Look at that young man, and observe how cleverly he sets about his work, and yet it was I who was his master, and initiated him in the knowledge of tactics." He had, in fact, given Louis Napoleon lessons in the art of war in Rome; and was now proud of his pupil.

While everything was in extreme uncertainty, Hortense, in an obscure inn at Foligno, walked to and fro in her chamber. The walls were dirty, and covered with smoke, and here and there on the plaster were inscriptions written by travellers as a reminiscence of their passage through the town; perhaps the only signs remaining to show that they had ever existed. She was very sad. Her imagination went back twenty years, to the birth of the King of Rome, when Napoleon was in the height of his power. She took up a pencil, and also wrote upon the wall, and while she was thus engaged her eldest son breathed his last. The courier she had despatched in search of the young men found them at Forli. The insurgents had already quitted

Bologna, threatened by the Austrian army, then on its march towards Ravenna.

On receiving this intelligence, Hortense found it impossible to remain any longer at Foligno, and set out on the road to Forli. At the very first post, however, a man approached her carriage, bringing her the disastrous news that Napoleon was dangerously ill, words which were soon exchanged for others still more disastrous, — that he was dead. During a whole day and a night, this unhappy mother travelled alone in search of sons of whom one was now no more. She arrived at length at Pesaro, where, overcome with fatigue, excitement, and grief, she betook herself to the palace of her nephew, and was carried more dead than alive to bed. Here Louis Napoleon came to her, and embracing her as sons in deep sorrow embrace their mothers, confessed that he was henceforward alone in the world, that his brother, his best and only friend, had died in his arms.*

---

* Louis Blanc speaks of his death as mysterious, but in what sense I am unable to decide. No doubt very great uncertainty hangs over it. We know very little of the circumstances which attended the young man's illness, or in what manner he breathed his last. It only seems clear that Louis never quitted his brother, but behaved towards him with the utmost affection while affection could be of any avail.

This might have appeared sufficiently calamitous for a mother. But immediately afterwards events occurred which made her look upon the speedy death of her son as a blessing from heaven. Had he lingered longer it would have been necessary to drag him about dying in her carriage, pursued by the enemy, and every moment in danger of falling into their hands. Nothing was now to be thought of but flight. The revolutionary authorities of Bologna had already taken refuge in Ancona, where, on the brink of the Adriatic, they were awaiting their fate. At no great distance in the rear, the Austrians, the most ferocious and relentless soldiers in Europe, were rapidly coming up. The Podesta of Pesaro now came to Hortense and said : " The enemy are almost in sight, and the sails of their ships are likewise visible in the offing, making towards Sinigaglia."

This was enough. Ill or well, living or dying, she must take instantly to flight. She had still one son left, and must endeavour to save him at all hazards. Horses were procured, and fastened at once to her carriage, into which she was lifted, not being able to walk. In this state she set out, reached Fano by nightfall, and on the morrow found herself in Ancona. The possessions of the Bonaparte family were widely scattered over this part of

Italy. Here also her nephew possessed a palace, on the very edge of the sea, the waves of which often leaped up to the window of the room she occupied. From this window, she could command a view of the whole port, and of the few frail barks in which alone the fugitive Republicans could possibly fly from the shores of Italy. Those wretched vessels constituted also her only hope, exposed as they would be to the ships of Austria, now complete masters of the Adriatic. To escape by land, she believed to be impracticable ; since, in the attempt to reach Foligno, she would have to penetrate through the Austrian lines with her unhappy son, who with General Zucchi and the Modenese had been excepted from the general amnesty proclaimed by the Austrian general upon entering the Papal territories.

Events distressing beyond description now succeeded each other without intermission. All foreigners who had joined the insurrection were to be put to death; there was therefore not a moment to be lost. This was the time to try the extent of her resources and the strength of her character. Looking far ahead she foresaw that should she even succeed in reaching the Tuscan territory, where it would be necessary for her to travel with the English passport, her progress would be inevitably stopped,

unless she could discover some one who would consent to·personate her eldest son.

Among those who were most deeply compromised
was the young Marchese Zappi. She sent for him,
and inquired whether he would place his life in
her hands. He consented, and preparations were
at once made for departure. While thus engaged she observed that Louis was not only sad and
melancholy, but extremely unwell. She sent for
a physician, who declared that he was in a fever, but
that if he went to bed at once, and were taken care
of, he might possibly be able to set out in the
morning. When the morning came, however, his
mother upon looking in his face saw it was covered
with a fiery eruption. He had the measles.

Hortense now stood in need of all her presence
of mind. · She caused a place to be taken on board
of a vessel still in the harbour; she sent for her son's
passport, signed by all the authorities, and made out
for Corfu; she spread the report that it was she
herself who was ill, and made up a bed for her son
in a cabinet close to her own room. Here she fell
on her knees, and almost in despair, threw her
whole soul on the protection of Providence. Her
servants went backwards and forwards between her
palace and the little vessel which was to weigh

anchor that evening for Corfu, and thus imposed
upon those persons whose curiosity led them to
busy themselves in these matters. Next day it
would have been too late; but the vessel set sail
at nightfall, and no one doubted that Louis Napoleon
had left the shores of Italy.

In truth, however, he still remained in the power
of his enemies; the slightest indiscretion might cause
his destruction. Everything was to be feared, and
in order to embarrass his mother still more a courier
arrived from her husband. Being himself in despair
he thought, of course, she had yielded to hers, and
vehemently insisted that Louis should embark immediately. " Save, I implore you," he said, " the only
son left to us." He then besought her to inform
him of all the arrangements which had been made,
but knowing the weakness of his character, she was
very careful not to comply with his wishes. Al-
lowing him to suppose with the rest of the world
that their son had set sail for Corfu, she began to take
measures for carrying out her own design. Scarcely
doubting that her husband's courier would be
stopped on the way, and the letters of which he
might be the bearer read, she dictated a letter to
her husband embodying the popular views respecting
her son. To use her own expression, she gave him

all the comfort he needed, and kept her troubles to
herself.   She said their son had set sail for Corfu *
with the passport made out in another name, that
he was in good health, that she felt no uneasiness
on his account, and that she would join him as soon
as she should be well enough to leave her bed.
When she found her husband had been terrified by
the intelligence that a ship bound from Ancona had
been taken by the Austrians, she got her son Louis to
write with his own hand a short letter dated Corfu,
in which he described his safe arrival, and said he
would write next from England.

The day after Louis fell ill, a courier came to
announce to Hortense that the Austrian general
would take up his quarters in the very palace in
which she was staying.   Here was a strange increase of the danger of her position, for although
she was not to be disturbed in the few rooms she occupied, a single door only divided her apartment

* This appears to have misled the public at the time, and
many writers since. M. Felix Wouters, for example, relates
without the least hesitation that he embarked, and in spite of the
Austrian squadron escaped out of the Adriatic.   Here, however,
his ideas become very confused, for instead of going to Corfu,
we are told he made the best of his way to France, and by
that route reached Switzerland in disguise ; p. 210.   It will be
seen, however, that Louis Napoleon's route was longer and
his dangers much greater than M. Wouters dreamt of.

from the chamber of the Austrian general. One of the principal objects of this man was to capture her son, who lay ill in the very next room to this his enemy. She was under the necessity, therefore, of forbidding him to speak, and when he coughed she ran and put her hand upon his mouth to prevent, if possible, the sound being heard. Austrian officers and soldiers meanwhile filled the palace, the court-yard, the staircases, and their harsh voices were heard all day uttering their grating dialect.

CHAP. IV.

PERILOUS RETREAT FROM ANCONA.

AT length, after eight days of anxiety and danger,
the physician declared Louis Napoleon to be in a
condition to travel. The decisive moment had then
arrived. How could he be got out of her bedroom,
out of the palace, out of Ancona? Trusting to
Providence, she ordered the horses to be got ready,
at the first peep of dawn, while she spread the
report that she would set out at seven. Of course
she did not sleep that night. One of her men servants
pretended to fall suddenly ill, and Louis Napoleon
put on his suit of livery; the Marchese Zappi, who
lay concealed at a friend's house, dressed himself in a
similar suit, and was in readiness to start at the first
flush of light. At four o'clock in the morning, the
queen left her chamber, and passing through the ad-
jacent apartment, filled with the sleeping Austrians,
descended the great staircase, at the foot of which
the guard, without interruption, suffered her to pass.
It was scarcely day; she drove through the streets

of the city, and went on to the gate, where her
passports were examined, and with a palpitating
heart, found herself in the open country. Louis
Napoleon stood like a footman behind her carriage,
and the Marchese Zappi behind that of her femme-
de-chambre. The lady who travelled as her companion, as soon as they were on the great road, gilded
by the sun now rising over the Adriatic, began to
congratulate her on having got safely through this
first danger. But the mother's solicitude could not
be thus dispelled. She thought rather of the thousand
risks that still lay before them, as she bent her way
towards Loretto.

The Bonaparte family, together with all its in-
timate partisans, may almost be said to have a
superstition of its own. Even Napoleon himself
cherished the puerile superstition of believing he had
a destiny, a peculiar order of nature, established and
set apart for him. The other members of the family,
inferior in genius, in knowledge, in intelligence,
adopted the same notions, and repeated them without
ceasing, until their followers were completely in-
doctrinated. Hortense, however, had now reached
that age at which nearly all Frenchwomen become
devout; and therefore turned her face towards
Loretto, as millions of women had done before,

to seek among the folds of the Virgin's drapery, for. that consolation which ambition had denied her. Having stopped and prayed in the church, Hortense continued her journey. At Macerata, her son was recognised by a person sufficiently generous to keep the discovery to himself. At Tolentino, where there was a detachment of the invading army, the passport of the Austrian general, given her at Ancona, probably preserved their lives, in conjunction with the honourable conduct of the commandant at this place, who, when a wretched Italian came up and informed him that he recognised Louis Napoleon in disguise, replied, that he had not been stationed there to arrest any one, and that, besides, the Duchess of St. Leu's passports were perfectly regular.

Though worn out with fatigue, Hortense refused to pause in her journey until she had passed the last outposts of the Austrians, after which she stopped at a miserable little village. Still it was necessary for her to advance rapidly, surrounded as she and her son were with dangers. She pushed on in haste through Foligno and Perusia, where all signs of gaiety had now disappeared. The inhabitants, conscious of their republican demonstrations, awaited in terror the approach of the Austrians.

On nearing the Tuscan frontier, Hortense's anxieties and apprehensions redoubled. The Grand Duke was kind by nature, and friendly towards her and her children ; but his government, completely under Austrian influence, would never pardon Louis for having escaped its surveillance, to adopt a hostile cause. She determined therefore, if possible, to traverse the Tuscan frontier by night, and contrive to arrive at the first town about two o'clock in the morning. Her terrors were here augmented by an accident. Anticipating her arrival, the ministers had despatched a special commissary to the frontier, who having been all day engaged in scrutinising travellers, had now retired to sleep at a distant villa. For this reason she was told her passports could not be signed. She now became almost beside herself with alarm. Her son was everywhere known in Tuscany, and had actually been recognised at the last post. What was to be done ? As he stood there, with his mother, looking about him in the night, every word spoken by the postillion to the inferior agents of the police increased his anxiety. After a little reflection, Hortense determined to send her passport by the courier to the commissary of police, having first explained to him all he was to say.

Practically the commissary's absence turned out to be a fortunate accident; for this man, though informed that the queen was there, was desirous of finding some pretext for not returning at such an hour to his post, and said to the courier, " Will you swear to me, that her son is not with her? I have the most peremptory orders not to suffer him to enter Tuscany." The courier assured him that Louis Napoleon had gone on board ship at Ancona, and that the queen intended to embark at Leghorn in order to join him at Malta. " She wished to remain," he added, " about a fortnight in the neighbouring province, for the purpose of taking the mineral waters, being extremely ill."

The courier, with an air of complete innocence, asked the commissary to give him certain information, as if he himself had much to learn and nothing to conceal. But, as he expected, the worthy functionary knew nothing, having only arrived the day before with directions to examine the insurgents who might be allowed to pass through the Grand Duchy on their way to banishment. He again repeated that Louis Napoleon was expressly excluded. The courier persuaded him that Hortense intended to sleep at Camoscia, a place at no great

distance from the frontier. Thither, he observed, the
commissary might come in the morning, see the
queen, and satisfy himself that all was right. Overcome partly by the courier's logic, and partly by his
own drowsiness, he signed the paper, and the queen
with her son passed the frontier.

Terrified by what she had heard, Hortense did not
doubt that the commissary would arrive early next
morning at Camoscia, where it had, in fact, been
her intention to take a little rest. It now became
necessary however to continue the journey without
intermission, and on reaching Camoscia she ordered
horses to be hired for two days, intending not to
pause till she arrived at Sienna. But when persons
are in great difficulties circumstances often appear to
combine to redouble them. She was told there were
no horses to be got, and that they had therefore no
choice but to remain where they were. She felt
herself therefore compelled to await the coming on
of day, when her son, it was hardly to be doubted,
would be discovered and either sent back or delivered
up to his enemies.

Their situation was peculiarly painful. The auberge was filled with fugitives, who were proceeding
to take refuge in Corsica, and it was quite as necessary

for Louis Napoleon to guard against being recognised by them as by less friendly eyes. Devoured by fear and anxiety, Hortense remained in her carriage, waiting impatiently for the means of continuing her journey, while Louis Napoleon, himself fatigued, feeble from illness, dejected, sad, and almost regardless of life, threw himself on a heap of stones in the street, where he slept till morning.

The horses having rested for two hours, the grooms brought them up while it was yet dark. The owners had consented to take the queen on to a village where it was expected that others might be procured from the peasants. As they were moving along the beautiful valley of Chiana, the day began to break, and call forth one after another all the charms of nature. But persons flying for their lives have no eye for the picturesque. They encountered, however, no obstruction, but travelled on rapidly the whole day, and rested at night in a little village close to the mineral waters. The strength of Hortense was now completely exhausted, and but for this fortunate sleep, secured to her by intense fatigue, she felt persuaded she must have died on the road.

On this little frequented track they had changed drivers several times, so that all trace of her and her

M

son was lost. No one knew who she was, and
something like a sense of security returned to
them. Still she had to go through Sienna, through
which she had been in the habit of passing every
year on her way to Rome. And if her son should
be discovered travelling in disguise, they would
inevitably be entirely lost. It was necessary, therefore, for her still to use her Tuscan passport, to
traverse the city in broad day, and only to assume
her English name at some village far ahead.

Her son, however, being personally known at
Sienna, her fears lest he should be recognised were
great. Her intention at first was to send him round
the walls on the outside, but this plan was abandoned, when she reflected on the rocky nature of
the ground, and the probability that there would be
no road or path, so that he might lose his way and
be encountered by the police, who infested the whole
country, lying in wait for the fugitives. She therefore drove right into the city ; and while her passports
were being examined at the gate, Louis Napoleon
leaped from behind the carriage, and, plunging into
bye lanes, made with all possible speed towards
the street leading to the Florence gate.

Fresh difficulties and embarrassments, however,

arose. All the horses in the place were engaged for the Grand Duke, who was every moment expected to arrive. The city would then be filled with people from Florence who knew them. Even now she beheld numerous acquaintances, among others, several English travellers, most of whom would have recognised her son instantly, under any disguise. What was to be done? By dint of liberal offers, the man who had brought her thus far, consented to go on to the next stage, if she would agree to wait two hours to rest his horses.

Having no choice, she consented, but arranged that it should be at a small alehouse outside the walls. To frighten her still more, the principal street had been unpaved, so that she had to make a detour, at the risk of missing her son, who would probably go back to the gate in search of her, and there be taken. With trembling anxiety, therefore, she looked out of her carriage windows. When her terror had been wrought up to the highest pitch, she saw him come down the street. He sprang behind the carriage, they dashed out of the gate, and once more believed themselves in comparative safety.

Their intention was to take advantage of a cross road towards Pisa, but before they could reach it'

they perceived one of the carriages of the Grand
Duke approaching at a distance.   There was not
a moment to be lost.   They pushed on therefore
with redoubled vigour, and by turning a little aside
were enabled to escape observation.   Incidents no
less perplexing occurred to them at Pisa and Lucca,
where Hortense was to some extent known.

She had now assumed her English name, and
travelled with her English passport.   At Pietra
Santa, near which her son Napoleon had formerly
lived with his wife, she began to breathe more
freely.   People by degrees get used to dangers.
While remaining here, she went out with her son,
and walked gently towards the valley of Seravezza.
No spot in Italy is perhaps more beautiful.   It
unites the magnificence of Switzerland, with the
softness of the South — delicious vallies, marble
mountains, lofty spreading trees, glimpses of the
distant sea, and a sky of deep azure tinged towards
the horizon with the soft glow of evening.   Her
thoughts, like those of her son, were with the dead.
Here she persuaded herself it would be delightful
to pass what remained to her of life, plunged in
soft melancholy, and communing quietly with her
own ideas.   They proceeded until they came within

sight of the foundations of the house which young Napoleon had begun to build for himself. The grass was now springing up among the stones while he lay at rest in the church of Forli.

CHAP. V.

LOUIS NAPOLEON VISITS AND PLOTS IN ENGLAND.

FROM this point to their arrival in France, though
they ran many risks of being recognised, they encountered no obstacles, and were engaged in no
romantic incidents. They passed the frontier; they
arrived at Cannes, where Napoleon had disembarked
on his return from Elba, and having spent the night
there, proceeded on the following morning towards
Paris. It should be recollected that the members of
the Bonaparte family were by law exiled from
France, and forbidden to return on pain of death.
But Louis Napoleon and his mother entertained
little fear, even should they be discovered, that the
law would be put in force against them. They
perfectly knew that the civilisation of the period
would prevent it, though they might be arrested and
imprisoned, or compelled once more to quit the
country.

As I have already remarked, the general voice of
France was not at that time raised in favour of the

Bonaparte family. Hortense felt and anticipated this. Her sons had been invited by some to enter the country, but it was not the national voice; she regarded it as a mere intrigue, and dissuaded them from making the attempt. On reaching Paris, Louis Napoleon wrote a letter to the citizen king, which he read to his mother. She approved of its spirit, but objected to its being sent. However, she made known to Louis Philippe her being in Paris, and as her son had again fallen ill, requested permission to remain a few days.

She saw the old king and his family. Nothing could exceed their politeness or their insincerity. Louis Philippe was the prince of impostors; expressed the greatest sympathy for her ; regretted, as Louis XVIII. had done, the cruel necessity of keeping her out of France for a little time longer; but he assured her it should indeed be but a little time, for that he would exert himself to reconcile his ministers to the idea of her residing in the country. He offered her money, friendship, favour, anything but what she wanted. The greatest possible eagerness was meanwhile exhibited to hasten her departure for London, and at length, to ease his paternal mind, they set out.

Previously, however, she had gone on Sunday to

mass at the Church of St. Roche, in the Rue St.
Honoré, where, by accident, she sat next to M.
Lamartine, who was pointed out to her by the
Marchese Zappi. She had always admired his
writings, and now extended her admiration to the
man. What would she have said, could she have foreseen that he would one day be her son's competitor
for the Presidentship of the French Republic; that
the admission of the Bonaparte family into France
would be in part owing to his remissness; and that
he would have to repent in sackcloth and ashes all
his life this act of negligence or weakness.

On the 6th of May they left Paris, and went to
sleep at Chantilly, and in four days reached Calais,
crossed the Channel, and were on their way to
London. Here Louis Napoleon had another illness. He was attacked by the jaundice, and looked
all over as yellow as a guinea. It was sometime
before they could get accustomed to the liberty of
this country. They could no longer pass for
English people, and therefore their servants were
directed to say who they were, and to pretend that
they had just arrived from Malta by way of Ports-
mouth. It was immaterial to the innkeepers whence
they had come or whither they were going. The
use of passports was at an end as well as the neces-

sity of fabricating white lies. For the first time in her life Hortense could go where she pleased, return when she pleased, and, provided she paid her way, be certain of not being molested by any one. She confesses that she had nowhere met with so much politeness as in London, where she made the discovery that the liberty which is so much coveted by mankind is no vain word, but a powerful reality.

We who are used to it, find it perhaps impossible to estimate our freedom at its full value, but foreigners who have lived long among the restraints, the embarrassments, the petty surveillance, the oppression and despotism of the Continent, experience inexpressible delight when, on disembarking in England, they draw a long breath, and for the first time feel that they are at perfect liberty. Our society no doubt has its faults and our government its imperfections. But personally we are as much our own masters as men were in those ages when

"Wild in woods, the noble savage ran."

It is pleasant, through the reflections of others, to be made aware of this, and be possessed by the proud consciousness of being an Englishman. We hate servitude — we hate tyranny, and fortunately we have got rid of them all. Hortense, however, was more sensible than her son of this great blessing, and probably had she lived to be consulted, would have pleaded for the extension of it to France. Familiar with the great cities of the Continent she discovered a new character altogether in the English capital. She admired its splendid pavements, the brilliant lighting up of the streets, the elegance and cleanliness of the parks, the absence of palaces and public monuments, and the indications which everywhere presented themselves of ease and equality. For the first time she felt she was complete mistress of herself. If she went into a shop, everybody treated her with kindness. The workmen often took Louis by the hand, observing, " We are your friends now ; " and when they performed for him a little service sometimes refused to receive any payment. The name of old Napoleon was his passport to general consideration.

Talleyrand was then French ambassador in London, and that clever old fox thought it his duty to make inquiries about Hortense and her son. He sent, therefore, a friend to call on her, to whom she recommenced her ancient fictions, observing that she left Italy at Leghorn, and intended to return into Switzerland, probably by way of Belgium. Her passage through France and interviews with Louis

Philippe were, by the direction of that sage old
gentleman, concealed from Talleyrand. The entire
diplomatic body was now in commotion. It appeared that every descendant or relative of Napoleon
possessed the power of agitating the whole political
world.

Belgium was at that time in a state of great
excitement, and the diplomatists feared that the
citizens of Brussels might seize upon Louis Napoleon on his passage and make him king whether
he would or not. It was judged unsafe, therefore,
that he and his mother should pass through Belgium,
and accordingly Hortense relinquished the idea.
The question of course now was through what
country she should go? Talleyrand offered her
a passport, under a false name, through the north
of France, and after much negotiation and exhibition of Jesuitism this was the plan decided upon.
Meanwhile Louis Napoleon and his mother enjoyed
themselves in London, visited in the first circles,
and went down to spend some time with the Duke
of Bedford at Woburn Abbey. In all great cities
strangers are killed by being dragged about to see
sights, and they were taken to Hampton Court—
to the Tower—to the Tunnel—to Woolwich and
to Richmond. At length, to escape from all these

things they went down to reside quietly at Tunbridge Wells.

At first sight, and from the ordinary current of events, we might be tempted to imagine that this visit to England had no political character or significance. Apparently the mother and son were absorbed altogether by the courtesies and amusements of society. They visited, they chatted, they laughed, they ate dinners, they seemed to enjoy the aspect of the country; but in spite of these semblances they were all the while plunged up to the ears in a political conspiracy.

Honest Joseph, when offered a crown in America, had wrapped himself in the mantle of philosophy and declined the honour. It would be wrong, however, to infer from this that ambition was extinct in him. His imagination shrank at the prospect of vegetating at the foot of the Andes among half-castes and degenerate Spaniards, and longed to be again about the Tuileries, the Louvre, and the Champ de Mars. France was in fact the bright taper around which the Napoleonic moths longed to wheel and flutter, until it either scorched them to death, or lighted them to some more agreeable form of existence. At all events, Joseph having grown weary of acting the stoic in the vicinity of Philadelphia, had now come to London to plot against Louis Philippe. The discovery was soon made that the Napoleonists, as a party, were not strong in France; and, therefore, the idea suggested itself that it would be desirable to form a coalition with the Republicans, who, it was hoped, would suffer themselves to be duped into a delusive compact with their worst enemies.

Jacques Lafitte and Lafayette were won over, and several other Republicans of distinction repaired to London in the hopes of being able to ripen that notable scheme of fusion. Several generals in the army of Louis Philippe displayed considerable eagerness to betray their trust; but not being able to invent any reasonable pretext for visiting the English capital, they went clandestinely to Ostend, where Louis Napoleon met them. What was to have formed the basis of the new revolution does not appear. In all likelihood it would have been republican in name, but certainly Bonapartist in reality. About the mode of carrying it on Louis Napoleon and Joseph differed essentially, the former being desirous of pushing things at once to extremities, while the latter, with the characteristic timidity of age, sought all manner of pretexts for procrastination.

Meantime the conductors of the republican journal "La Tribune," having discovered the design of the conspirators, denounced it fiercely to the public. They went back over the history of the Revolution; they enumerated its chiefs, the victims of Napoleon's perfidy and despotism, and they earnestly cautioned the French people against being deluded a second time by any member of the Bonaparte family, against which they inveighed as a tyrannical cabal utterly irreconcileable with liberty. The conspirators attributed this proceeding to the machinations of Louis Philippe; but with whomsoever it originated, it sufficed to thwart the designs of the Bonapartes, and to postpone for nearly twenty years their advent to power.

A residence in England by no means suited the taste or the views of Hortense, whose home properly speaking was in Switzerland. She had not yet made up her mind, however, whether she should pass through Paris or avoid it. A conversation with her son decided her. "If the people should rise," he said, "I would not stand still and see them cut down before my face, but would certainly place myself among them."

Hortense then determined to spare him the embarrassment of such a situation, and to avoid the capital. As I was in Paris at the close of that summer, and moved a great deal in political circles, I think I may venture to say that his patriotism would not have been put to the proof. There had not yet been time for the people to grow tired of Louis Philippe, who, on the contrary, was in the zenith of his popularity. Everybody, from the marquis to the shopkeeper, boasted of his public spirit and winning manners. I saw him ride daily up the Avenue de Neuilly, with his wife and children, in an open carriage, displaying no state, and obviously experiencing no apprehensions of the populace.

It was his policy just then to affect the manners of a private gentleman, and the crowds were so charmed by his behaviour, that they stood in long lines beside the road, taking off their hats and cheering him vigorously as he passed. In return he bowed most graciously, showered benign smiles on everybody, and looked as if he could have embraced with all his heart the whole population of Paris. At that time, therefore, the avatar of a Bonaparte would have been far from welcome in the French capital; and Louis Napoleon, had he showed himself, would have made the unpleasant discovery that his sage and gallant countrymen preferred the pyriform visage of Louis Philippe to his own.

On the 7th of August, Louis Napoleon and his mother left England to return to Switzerland. They landed at Calais, and proceeded leisurely to Boulogne, where, as they stood on the summit of the column, surveying the town, the coast, and the blue waters of the Channel, replete for Hortense with melancholy associations, he probably conceived the first idea of the expedition, which eight years later he directed against that place.

On arriving at Chantilly they went to visit the palace of the Condés and the magnificent forest which, during the empire, had been her own property. On the edge of this forest I myself once resided with my family, and among its shady walks, and along the edge of its beautiful lakelets my children used to play in summer or toil through deep snow in winter. It was extremely natural that Hortense should wish to know whether or not she was still remembered in these parts where she had once been so powerful. She inquired of the man who drove them through Chantilly and its vicinity, to whom those woods formerly belonged. He replied, to Queen Hortense, and added, that for many years she was supposed to roam about the forest in disguise, but that for some time people had ceased to talk of her. " Ah, without doubt she is dead," replied the queen, and the idea pleased her, finding she was forgotten.

After wandering about reviving reminiscences at every step, Hortense and her son moved on to St. Denis, and afterwards through a number of places, in many, if not in most, of which she had seen happier days. In company with his mother, Louis Napoleon visited Ermenonville and Morfontaine, places in which she had once been happy with her mother Josephine. A rickety old boat took them over at Ermenonville to the Isle of Poplars, consecrated to the memory of Rousseau, where she and her son inscribed their names upon his tomb. On her way she went to visit the grave of her mother, which she found freshly strewn with flowers. There were, then, those who still remembered Josephine ; it was her daughter only who was forgotten. Malmaison had been sold to a rich proprietor, who had allowed it to fall into ruins. Even places consecrated by the most illustrious dead are often not greatly respected by the living, and in the case of Josephine there was, in truth, not very much to venerate , still her daughter could not otherwise than blame those who allowed her cherished residence to fall into decay.

N

Pursuing their journey without interruption, they arrived in due time at the Château of Arenenberg, where they enjoyed some repose after the two stormy years they had passed in Italy, France, and England.

CHAP. VI.

SHIFTS THE SCENE OF HIS POLITICAL OPERATIONS TO SWITZERLAND.

Louis Napoleon young as he was, had now acquired considerable experience of mankind, and some knowledge of politics. It has already been seen that he made profession of republican principles, and really perhaps imagined himself an advocate of the rights of mankind. He had passed through a period of fierce action, he had conspired; he had set cardinals, popes, and kings, at defiance; he had fought; he had aided those who liberated twenty thousand political prisoners from the fortresses and dungeons of Romagna; and he now therefore thought himself qualified to sit down calmly and write " Political Reveries " and " Considerations on the state of Switzerland "

But it is easier to fight bravely than to think originally. Louis Napoleon had courage, strong aspirations after power, and very little respect for the established order of things in any part of the world. His ideas, however, were rather those of his family than his own, besides, the " Rêveries," which have often

been spoken of as a book, were only a few slight
thoughts thrown carelessly together, and indicating
the writer's strong desire to exercise power over the
French people. Châteaubrand, who happened to be
then on a visit at the Château of Arenenberg,
looked over the manuscript and suggested several
alterations, some of which were probably adopted,
though the paper containing his suggestions having
got mislaid, the author failed to derive from them all
the benefit which he might otherwise have done. In
a little piece entitled " The Exile," there is a passage
which should be whispered nightly to the author's
ear, by many thousand voices from the burning
sands of Africa and the pestilential marshes of
Cayenne.

" Oh, you whom happiness has rendered selfish,
who have never suffered the tortures of exile, you
think it a slight thing to banish a man from his
country ; you have to learn that exile is a perpetual
martyrdom, that it is death, — not the glorious death
of those who die for their native land, not the still
sweeter death of those whose last breath is breathed
forth beside the domestic hearth, but a death of
wasting away, slow and hideous, which undermines
you, hour by hour, until it at length lays you low in
an obscure and desert grave."

If I conversed with Louis Napoleon, I would re-
mind him of these words, and of all those others
scarcely less forcible and eloquent which succeed
them in the fragment.   When he wrote them he was
himself an exile, and experienced all the bitterness of
his condition.   Would it not be politic now to throw
open freely the approaches to France to those thousands of brave men who must otherwise be gathered
to their fathers in those distant and nameless graves
which he has described so well.

Every person who bore the name of Bonaparte
thought himself constrained to favour revolution, not
for the purpose of liberating nations, but as a means
of self-aggrandisement.   This was pre-eminently
Louis Napoleon's case : he looked down from the
Swiss mountains upon the rich plains of France, and
conceived, not without some reason, that the terres-
trial level before him represented pretty correctly
the intellectual level of the nation.   There was
nothing very great to be seen anywhere.   In the
reunions of the Bonaparte clan, he had no doubt
learned one very important lesson, namely, that of
keeping his mind free from the vulgar superstition of
titles and distinctions.   He looked upon a king as a
man, and nothing more.   He therefore entertained
very little respect for Louis Philippe, whose dis-

honesty, political hypocrisy, mock piety, and real irreligion, inspired him with contempt. Still he beheld the regal Tartuffe imposing successfully upon the world.

But there was another superstition in France, to which he now began seriously to think of addressing himself. I mean that superstition of the French military classes for his uncle's memory, which really partook of the nature of idolatry. He bethought himself too of another circumstance little less significant or important — the influence of the Roman Catholic clergy and the Jesuits over the minds of the people. Louis Philippe was a materialist, and favoured what the French were then pleased to call philosophy, which means hostility to all that is spiritual and noble in our nature. He surrounded his dynasty with freethinkers, scoffers, men without faith or truth, whose principal delight in life was turning religion into ridicule. Napoleon had done the same, and reaping as he had sown, found among the men of his own ideas, innumerable examples of baseness, treachery, and ingratitude. It seemed to Louis Napoleon that without being religious, it would be possible, by affecting a respect for the Church, to secure the co-operation of the clergy; he therefore became, it is said, a member of the Society of Jesus, which, though attached to the Bourbons, would not

object to the Bonapartes, provided that through them
they could increase the lustre and power of their
order.

Hortense, as I have already remarked, had entered
upon the devout period of life, loved to visit churches,
to pray before images and to interest the hierarchy
in the fate of her son.   He had been brought up, it
will be remembered, by an abbé; he had an uncle in
the sacred college; his grandmother had been a sort
of femlae pope at Rome.   All his traditions therefore,
all his connexions, all his ideas were impressed with
the character of the papacy.   This was something to
begin with; still his visible and palpable inheritance
was his uncle's fame.   Upon that, it would always
be safe to trade in France.

Philosophers compliment man with the reputation
of being a thinking animal.   But in reality very few
men think at all   The things which pass through
their minds, and obtain the name of thoughts or
ideas, are mere phantasms, prejudices, fallacies,
puerile opinions, which it demands no effort
to receive or to perpetuate.   People in such a
mental state are ready to worship anything, and
these constituted the mass of Napoleon's partisans.
Louis therefore very judiciously addressed himself in
his writings to this large section of the French

people; but, not possessing the art of interesting their imaginations, he might have continued writing till doomsday, without producing any impression on them, for in spite of the name upon the title-page, the world would not read his books. There was nothing new, nothing great, nothing absorbing in his ideas. What he wrote was not amiss. In his opinions, he was sometimes right, though very often wrong. But it was always the old Napoleon material that was worked up; a thin film of republicanism on the surface concealed the deep stratum of imperialism which lay solid and compact below.

Failing to move the world by his pen, Louis Napoleon essayed to move it by acting on the fancy of women. It is well known that the gentler sex are in general fond of titles, and very much carried away by respect for dynasties. Louis therefore now began to think of what could be done by making love, not as a matrimonial speculation, but as a means of creating partisans. Nature had denied him manly beauty, but fortune had made him a prince, and fortune in this instance was too powerful for nature. He went out into society, he made himself friends, he laid himself out for travellers, he became talked of, and every mention made of him, augmented his influence over the French mind.

Our neighbours are a very gallant people, very
philosophical, and very witty, but nevertheless it is
extremely easy to dupe them. Besides they have a
habit of getting tired of everything. Louis Philippe,
moreover, was growing old, and had all the vices
which nature too often connects with age. He was
greedy of money, and there were few things of which
he would not be guilty to obtain it. Like Napoleon
also, he wished to quarter his sons and daughters, as
kings and queens, upon all the surrounding countries.
He was always intriguing, always meddling with the
funds, always filling his bags, and emptying other
people's.

Charles V. describes fortune as a true woman,
who leaves the old to smile upon the young, and
Louis Napoleon confidently reckoned upon finding
her in this mood. Military adventurers, in whom
France always abounds, came to him from time to
time, assuring him of the attachment of the army,
and demonstrating how easy it would be for a man
of courage and capacity with all the pretensions
which he possessed, to make his appearance on any
point of the frontier, win over a small number of
regiments, and with these to march upon the capital
and leaven the whole army with revolution.
Napoleon's triumphant march upon Paris, after his

return from Elba, was too obvious not to be cited as an example of what might be done. Of course there was this difference, that Louis was not his uncle, and had not led the soldiers to victory on a hundred fields. Still it might be worth while to try what could be accomplished. To organise an insurrection was something better than writing common-place books, spinning political reveries, or political considerations, and waiting until fortune should come across the troubled waters of this world, like the dove to the ark, bringing along with her a laurel instead of an olive leaf.

These reflections maturely weighed at length decided him, and he determined to commence his career by making a dash upon Strasbourg. Many persons have called in question the morality of this enterprise as well as of that afterwards undertaken against Boulogne. But in my opinion, it was by no means more immoral than the return of the Bourbons to France. He had as much right as any one else to make himself master of the throne, if he could succeed in getting it. If he had no just claim, neither had Louis XVIII., nor had Louis Philippe. He merely invited the French people to make a new choice of a king or emperor. If they chose him, well, he would gain a crown. If not, he had a head

at the service of Louis Philippe, who was free to cut
it off if he pleased. It must have been by some
such logic as this that Louis Napoleon convinced
himself of the justice and practicability of his enterprise. In the mere matter of prudence, he was
inferior to the Bourbons, as well as to Louis
Philippe. The former had been forced upon France
by foreign bayonets; the latter had owed his throne
to his own intrigues, to the weakness of Lafayette,
to the precipitation and caprice of the Parisians.
Louis Napoleon appealed likewise to bayonets, but
they were at least French, and so far, I think, he
was more respectable than Louis XVIII. or his
successors.

The country in which Louis Napoleon had found
an asylum had been recently engaged in a quarrel
with France, which, always addicted to the system
of espionage, had been supporting a gang of emissaries
on the Swiss territory, thus insulting the dignity of
the Republic. But France was powerful, and
Switzerland was weak. In the eyes of Louis
Philippe, it mattered not at all on which side justice
lay. It was sufficient for him that he possessed the
means of overawing the confederated cantons, and
the insolence of his ambassador proved that he relied exclusively on force. The cantons submitted,

but the whole population of Switzerland cherished in their hearts the most inveterate hatred against the government which had subjugated their own.

It was while matters were in this situation between Switzerland and France that Louis Napoleon organised his conspiracy. When the plan first suggested itself to him is not known, but probably it dates as far back as the revolution of July. Up to that time he may have thought with the rest of the world that the government of the Restoration was calculated to be durable, as it really was had the Bourbons known how to accommodate themselves to the genius of the age. Their fall is a proof of how absurd the attempt is to govern by obsolete ideas. Louis XVIII. and Charles X. never reflected that they were living in the nineteenth century. Their minds were filled with the traditions of Louis XIV., and they considered the French nation, with the country it inhabited, as entirely their property, and repudiated all notions of liberty, right, and justice as puerile innovations.

The overthrow of such a government was as natural as it was easy; and Louis Napoleon never forgave himself for the misfortune of not having been on the spot to pick up the crown which had been cast into

the streets of Paris in the month of July. It seems
to me perfectly certain that from that day forward
his whole life was a conspiracy, and numbers of
officers in the French army, despising Louis
Philippe's political inaction, were easily gained over
by the agents of Louis Napoleon. He further took
means to discover the state of parties in France, the
inclinations of leading statesmen, and the general
temper of the army. The reports of his friends were
neither altogether favourable nor altogether the
reverse; but, upon carefully balancing chances, it
appeared to him that there existed good reasons for
auguring well of an attempt at a military insurrection. His greatest fears were of the republican
party, which, in France, however, is the most unintelligible of political combinations. It is not based
so much on patriotism as on ambition. Real Republicans do not desire the subversion of governments,
that they may personally profit by it, but that their
country may become greater and happier. In France
it is to be feared the word republic has been too often
used to mask designs of personal aggrandisement,
either in politics or war.

Louis Blanc, who professedly belongs to this party,
observes that, at the time of which I am speaking, it

was compelled to defer its hopes, for want of a name and a chief. This remark of itself suffices, because it is founded in truth, to explain the failure of republican efforts among our neighbours. When the people require a name and a chief, they may be prepared for insurrection, for barricades, for war, for glory, for conquest, but they are not prepared for a Republic. This means the abnegation of self, hostility to the worship of great names and great personages, and an ardent love of liberty for its own sake. Yet they who considered themselves republicans at that time in France were formidable, because they were brave, and ready to shed their blood like water for what they called liberty, equality, fraternity, symbolised by the tri-coloured flag.

Louis Napoleon therefore might well fear them, and desire to win them over to his side, as he afterwards, with the greatest ability, contrived to do, for their entire destruction and his own aggrandisement. For this result several democratic writers of eminence are partly answerable. They laboured to bring about the recal of the Bonaparte family; they exhausted their remarkable abilities in impressing upon the minds of the French people the belief of Louis Napoleon's goodness; and they are now expiating their mistake by an exile which will be co-lasting with their lives, or at least with Louis Napoleon's power, unless they choose to abjure their principles, and consent to write in the interest of a master.

/

CHAP. VII.

HIS FIRST ATTEMPT AGAINST LOUIS PHILIPPE'S THRONE.

WHEN Louis Napoleon had in theory matured his design, he proceeded to Baden-Baden, nominally in search of pleasure, but in reality for the purpose of finding fit instruments to work with. How far on this or any other occasion Hortense was acquainted with her son's designs does not very distinctly appear; but it seems to me that she knew more of them than is generally imagined. When he left her at Arenenberg, ostensibly to proceed on a hunting party into the principality of Heckingen, she displayed far more excitement and emotion than would have been called forth by the prospect of a separation of a few weeks. It seems evident that she understood the full extent of the danger he was about to encounter; for throwing her arms about his neck, she pressed him to her heart, and then slipped upon his finger the marriage ring of Napoleon and Josephine, which she regarded as a sort of talisman calculated to protect him in the hour of peril. No mother acts thus, when her son is merely going to enjoy the pleasures of the chase, and Hortense certainly would not have indulged in any such extravagance ; but if she understood the nature of the design which took him from her, and that he was going to strike for empire or death, the profoundness of her emotion was both natural and justifiable.

A knowledge of the conspiracy had already begun to be diffused through those classes of French society which are most deeply infected with the passion for change. There are in all countries those who love mystery, intrigue, excitement for their own sake, and who will venture or lose their lives rather than remain in that state of stagnation, which to persons of an ambitious character is worse than death. There was at this time, hovering about the confines of the political world, a certain Madame Gordon, the daughter of a captain in the imperial army, by profession a public singer. To her the secret of the conspiracy was by chance disclosed, upon which she threw herself impetuously into the design, and coming in a professional way to Baden-Baden made known to Louis Napoleon the fact of her having been initiated.

To what extent she now became mixed up with

O

his projects, it is not easy to decide. She had many patrons, friends, admirers, and devoted herself altogether to the winning over of new partisans to the Pretender. Other individuals, apparently more influential, but in reality perhaps of inferior consequence, joined the conspiracy, actuated partly by dislike of Louis Philippe's lethargic government, partly by that mental intoxication which urges political adventurers to engage in desperate enterprises simply for the gratification they afford the craving mind.

Among these was Colonel Vaudrey, who commanded at Strasbourg the fourth regiment of artillery. The basis of a revolution was now laid down with considerable ability. The first step was to win over the democrats of Alsace, by holding out to them the hopes of calling the people lawfully together; to allure the garrison of Strasbourg with the cry of Vive l'Empereur, to call the people to liberty, and the youth of the public schools to arms, to place the fortifications under the care of the national guard, and then, at the head of all the military force that could be collected, to march upon Paris. It was not doubted that at the sight of the imperial eagle the old soldiers who had conquered in so many wars would leave the plough, and hasten to aid in the construction of a new empire.

But when men deal with calculations, they find
everything easy. It is different when they descend
to realities. In order to judge for himself of his
chances of success, Louis Napoleon repaired to
Strasbourg, where, on calling his friends together,
and entering with them into deliberation, his enthusiasm was damped. Some of those to whom he addressed himself, betrayed his designs to the public
authorities, and it appeared that among the individuals immediately about him was an agent of the
government. No doubt this man was one of the
most ardent of the conspirators, because he was at
once commissioned to excite and to betray. He
urged Louis Napoleon to his ruin, affecting all the
while to be his bosom friend; he took down his
words, he registered his looks and gestures, and old
Louis Philippe, in his snug cabinet in the Tuileries,
chuckled over the wild projects of the ambitious
youth whom he coaxed into rebellion that he might
have a pretext for crushing him.

Let me not however be understood to attribute
the origin of the Strasbourg expedition to Louis
Philippe. The idea sprang from the mind of Louis
Napoleon himself, but the moment it became visible
the French Government had an emissary by his
side. The history of this expedition has been too

often written, to render it either interesting or necessary to enter with minuteness into details.   Louis
Napoleon having repaired to Strasbourg, concealed
himself in the house of M. Persigny, where he remained till considerably after dark.   He then left his
effects and papers in the charge of Madame Gordon
and proceeded to another house in a distant part of
the city, in which at a certain hour all the conspirators were to assemble on the ground floor.   The
weather was cold, but a bright autumnal moon lighted
up the streets of Strasbourg, whose gloomy build-
ings were converted by the force of his imagination
into so many harbingers of success.

All the arrangements practicable had been carefully made, but in such undertakings the interval
which immediately precedes the final blow is replete
with so keen a sense of danger, and beset with so
many solicitudes that even at the risk of shipwreck-
ing their design, the accomplices are under a sort of
necessity of meeting, deliberating, and encouraging
each other.   They sat in consultation all night,
meaning to strike the decisive blow at six o'clock in
the morning.   No one in the house knew why these
persons had met together, or what reasons they
could have for sitting up so late.

At length the other lodgers went to bed, and it is
probable that in the whole house the conspirators

only remained awake. But when men are playing
at so desperate a game, and have set down their
lives as the stake, the animal spirits are too much
excited to render sleep possible. A short time
before day, the tramp of horse soldiers was heard in
the street, and the members of the little plot, imagining themselves to be discovered, ran to the window,
threw it open and looked out. In a French country
town, the streets at night are indescribably dark
and dreary, especially on the verge of November.
The prospect which met their eyes was cold and dis-
couraging, and the noise and clatter still continuing,
one of their number went forth to reconnoitre.
While he was absent their solicitude and apprehensions increased ; but after keeping them in suspense
he returned, and explained that the cause of their
alarm had been a small body of troopers sent out
from the cavalry barracks in search of some run-
away horses. The noise they had made during
their excitement awakened the people over head,
who also went to the window, and had they listened
might probably have heard enough to compromise
the conspirators But they returned to their beds,
and left Louis Napoleon and his friends waiting
anxiously for the six o'clock chimes.

At length the bells in the old cathedral tower begin

to announce to the good Catholics of Strasbourg
that the hour of devotion had arrived. The conspirators emerged into the streets which were still obscure,
and proceeded towards the barracks of the artillery.
Just as the dim light of dawn was creeping down
between the tall houses of Strasbourg, the men of
the fourth regiment were called out into the open
space before their cantonments, where Colonel Vaudrey, with his drawn sword in his hand, exclaimed
to them, "Behold the nephew of Napoleon," upon
which the men, with as much enthusiasm as they
could muster on a cold autumnal morning, exclaimed
"Vive l'Empereur!"

There were, however, many other regiments in
garrison at Strasbourg, which it was necessary to
gain over, together with their commander General
Voirol. Towards his apartments, Louis Napoleon,
Colonel Vaudrey, and their friends now proceeded,
and breaking into his chamber found him still un-
dressed. Holding up before his eyes the eagle
which they bore along with them, they invited him
to recognise the symbol of the empire, and join
their enterprise. General Voirol, however, instead
of giving his assent, endeavoured to convince Louis
Napoleon of the hopelessness of his undertaking, and
his words, delivered with decision and authority, cast

a damp over their enthusiasm; placing him under arrest, they proceeded with a considerable abatement of confidence towards the barracks to harangue the troops.

Throughout this affair, Louis Napoleon displayed much courage, but very little sagacity. He suffered himself to be led up a narrow lane, into a small square, from which there was no other exit. But little time was left for reflection; every moment was precious, retreat was hardly to be thought of, and yet affairs were already beginning to wear an unpromising aspect. The artillerymen stood behind their guns, to which the horses were already limbered, and it is probable, that had time been allowed for their passions to warm, they might have fired upon the infantry and commenced a civil war in the streets. But the several regiments of foot then in garrison at Strasbourg received Louis Napoleon coldly. They raised no shout; no exciting cry passed from rank to rank. Some one exclaimed, ' It is not the nephew of Napoleon, but Colonel Vaudrey's own nephew, I know him well, for I have studied with him."

This produced sneers and laughs of derision among the soldiers, and Louis Napoleon saw in an instant that his hopes were at an end. Still

he once or twice attempted to address the soldiers,
but perceiving it to be all in vain, he besought
one of the artillerymen to give him a horse, on
which he might save himself by flight. It was to
no purpose. His enemies closed round him. He
retreated towards a wall, numbers of the infantry
with fixed bayonets pursuing. The artillery horses
scared by the noise and the flash of sabres reared
and plunged, and the future emperor ran imminent
risk of being trampled to death in an ignominious
fray. It now at length became evident that no
amount of intrepidity could any longer avail, so with
as good a grace as he could command, he yielded
himself up a prisoner to the soldiers, and soon found
ample leisure to collect his ideas in one of the
dungeons of Strasbourg.

It generally happens, that conspirators commit
their designs to writing, set down their names and
numbers, and fabricate documents calculated to compromise all their friends and adherents, who, but
for these proofs, might escape suspicion. Louis Napoleon had fallen into this grievous error, and left at
his lodgings heaps of letters and papers full of fatal
evidence against his fellow-conspirators. In a small
city like Strasbourg, news spreads like wild fire.
Madame Gordon soon learned the failure of the

enterprise; but instead of providing for her own safety by flight, she employed herself in committing hastily to the flames all the memorials of the plot. This act of courage and sagacity on the part of a woman defeated the vengeance of the French Government, and preserved many who must otherwise have shared the ruin of Louis Napoleon's cause. The men in authority under Louis Philippe were not permitted to behave insolently or harshly towards their prisoner.

Having been kept in confinement for several days, he was informed that a carriage was in waiting at the door, in which he was to proceed to Paris. None of his friends were allowed to accompany him; all were left to face the rigour of the law, while his rank, and the relation in which he stood to a former dynasty, preserved him from being treated as a common political offender.

Hortense in this emergency once more quitted her retreat at Arenenberg, and in spite of the decree of banishment, which still existed in all its rigour against her, ventured into France, to intercede with Louis Philippe for her son. It was not consistent with this wily monarch's policy to put to death a pretender to the throne. In less than two hours after his arrival in Paris Louis Napoleon was on his road to L'Orient, where a frigate lay at anchor to bear him to the United States. It is said that on this occasion he wrote a letter to Louis Philippe, expressing his gratitude for the clemency which had been shown him, and pledging himself never again to make any attempt against the French Government. But as no such letter has ever been produced by the partisans of the House of Orleans, it may fairly enough be presumed that none was written.

History is not a series of libels whether against the fortunate or against the unfortunate. Louis Napoleon was perfectly justified in thanking Louis Philippe for sparing his life, and granting him also his liberty, let the motives which prompted to this conduct have been what they might. But he was always too little impulsive—too cautious—too cold to be easily betrayed into making written promises which he could not but know would either fetter his conduct during his whole life, or expose him to the charge of perfidy and ingratitude. Whatever he said to the chief of the house of Orleans was probably said orally. Such language in certain circumstances is supposed by the Jesuitical moralists not to be binding.

> " He that imposes an oath makes it,
> Not he who for convenience takes it ;
> So how can any man be said
> To break an oath he never made ? "

Louis Napoleon emphatically denies the fact; but in the act of doing so falls into a strange confusion of ideas, from which it would not be unfair to infer that there were circumstances connected with this transaction which he desired to conceal. His words are — " They could not prevail upon me to sign an engagement, since I demanded to be left in prison; besides they never sought to make me do so." The reasoning which appears to be implied in this passage is extremely illogical. The words " they could not make me sign" imply that they tried and failed. And why did they fail? because he demanded to remain in prison. If no proposition had been made to him, to what was this demand a reply? Was it said apropos of nothing? When Louis Napoleon wrote these words, he must have possessed great faith in the credulity of mankind, for the words, " I demanded to be left in prison," clearly imply that some proposal had been made to him to deliver himself from captivity which did not meet with his approval. Yet he immediately adds that no endeavour of any kind was made to induce him to enter into any engagement. Colonel Vaudrey, to whom these words were written, may have understood them, but I confess I don't.

CHAP. VIII.

CROSSES THE ATLANTIC.

WHOEVER studies without prejudice the life of
Louis Napoleon must be inspired with admiration
by the steadiness and consistency with which he has
pursued the great purpose of his life.   He measured
the distance between his position as an adventurer and
an exile and the imperial throne of France, and determined that nothing should be wanting on his part
to narrow the interspace and render the passage
easy.   His great instrument always was the impression left upon the French mind by Napoleon.
With this he worked, upon this he reposed his
hopes.

When condemned to transportation he remained
ten days in the citadel of Port Louis, waiting for a
fair wind.   The authorities, through a sense of duty,
or in obedience to positive orders, visited him daily,
and he either saw, or pretended to see, in their language and demeanour strong proofs of attachment
to the memory of Napoleon.   It was his policy to

discover everywhere indications of the existence of this sentiment, and when he did not find it he carefully sought by the ease and popularity of his manners to inspire it.

On the 21st of November, 1836, the sub-prefect of L'Orient, entering the citadel, informed him that the frigate was ready to set sail. The drawbridge of the fortress was let down, and accompanied by the magistrates and the officers of the gendarmerie he passed out between two lines of soldiers stationed there to keep back the crowd which had collected to see the nephew of the emperor going into banishment. For a moment this circumstance afforded him some gratification, but when he mounted the frigate's deck and observed the shores of France growing dim and disappearing in the distance he experienced that contraction of the heart which most men feel when bidding an adieu which may prove eternal to their native land.

On board the frigate, the utmost care appears to have been taken to provide for his comforts. The captain, M. de Villeneuve, a regular old sailor, gave him the best cabin; he dined with the principal officers and with two curious passengers who were proceeding for very different purposes to Brazil. One of these, Don Pedro's librarian, a stiff courtier of the old school, was going out to lodge complaints against the Brazilian Government for having subjected him to ill treatment; the other, a savant of twenty-six, full of superstition and conceit, was sent out by Louis Philippe to make experiments in electricity. Secretly Louis Napoleon regarded him with well merited contempt. He believed in magnetism, and affected to possess the power to foretell future events. Of course he undertook to prophesy agreeably for his fellow-passenger, and in order to keep up the spirits of the exile, predicted that a member of Napoleon's family would soon appear in France and dethrone Louis Philippe.

It would be a good speculation for any rich pretender to keep as many prophets and soothsayers as possible in his pay, for no class of men act so powerfully on the public mind and prepare the way for revolutions. Everybody laughs at them outwardly, but their mysterious words sink deep into weak minds, and gradually direct into the desired channel the current of the nation's beliefs and sympathies. Few are proof against the perpetual predictions of skilful and intrepid soothsayers.

It was nearly a fortnight before the frigate could get out of the Channel. Rough and contrary winds kept it rocking about perpetually on the waves,

without power to make the slightest way; but at
length the weather proving more favourable it put
out into the Atlantic, where the captain opened his
sealed orders. But the giving of such instructions
was in this instance a mere farce, since they had on
board two passengers who were known to be bound
for Brazil. The only point on which Captain
Villeneuve may not have been previously informed
was, that Louis Napoleon instead of being taken
directly to New York was to make the voyage to
Rio Janeiro, where he was to be kept safely on
board during the re-victualling of the ship, and afterwards to be conveyed to the United States. As
the frigate was on its way to the South Sea, this
curious arrangement augmented the length of its
voyage by three thousand miles, but the climate of
South America being somewhat unhealthy, Louis
Philippe may have thought it would multiply his
chances of delivering himself from a disagreeable
rival.

Louis Napoleon, when he writes of his own
feelings and opinions, writes well. He appears to
have been always accustomed to reflect upon the
movements of his own mind, upon his sensations,
upon his hopes and fears. He is a reader of
Châteaubriand and Jean-Jacques Rousseau, and

sometimes writes in the manner of one, sometimes
in that of the other.   Among the great faults of
his enemies is the determination not to recognise
the power of thinking and writing which he undoubtedly possesses.   Authors who would be extremely unwilling to be thought guilty of prejudice
and partiality have suffered themselves nevertheless
to be misled by their political antipathies.   But,
after all, self-respect and the consideration of what
you owe to the public compel you to acknowledge
that justice is due to every man, tyrant or slave.   I
repeat, then, that Louis Napoleon, when he writes of
himself, of his sentiments, of his affections, of the
incidents and circumstances of his life, displays no
ordinary ability.   His style becomes animated,
picturesque, touching.   He carries your sympathies
along with him, and makes you acknowledge that,
in certain situations, he has meditated, and reflected,
and felt like a man of integrity and heart.

Writing to his mother from within the tropics,
he says, " We have got through the winter, and are
again in the midst of summer," though it was only
the middle of December.   " To the storms of the
North, have succeeded the trade winds, which allow
me to remain as much as I please on deck.   Seated
on the poop, I reflect on what has happened to me,

and think of Arenenberg and you. Our situations
are greatly modified by the affections of our minds ;
two months ago, my strongest desire was never to
return to Switzerland; and now, if I were free to
follow my own inclinations, I would fly eagerly back
to it, and sit down once more in that little room
overlooking the beautiful country in which I fancy
I ought to have been so happy. But when we feel
strongly it is generally our lot to be overwhelmed
by the weight of inaction, or in the convulsions of
painful situations."

He then alludes to a circumstance which has been
little noticed by his biographers. "When, some
months ago," he says, "I was bringing home Ma-
thilde, we entered the park together, and beheld
there a tree which had just been shattered by a
storm; upon which I said within myself that
our marriage would in like manner be broken off
by fate. What at that time presented itself to my
mind vaguely has been since realised. Have I then
during this year exhausted all the little stock of happiness which has been allotted me in this world ?"

To this question I will not undertake to furnish
any reply ; but I may be permitted to doubt whether,
as he sat there on the Atlantic surge, writing like an
affectionate son to his mother, he was not really in a

more enviable situation than any in which he has since been placed. He had not then sullied his mind by the bloody orgies of December and called up a nightmare which will hover over his conscience till death.

The young lady to whom he alludes in the above passage, the daughter of Jerome Bonaparte, was then little more than sixteen years of age, having been born at Trieste on the 27th May, 1820. She is described by some writers as a person of great beauty, small in figure, but perfectly formed, with a head of classical mould, large sparkling eyes, and regular features full of expression. But from this account it is necessary, according to others, to make a considerable abatement. She was probably very pretty in early youth, when her complexion was in its bloom, and her light brown hair in all its luxuriance. But soon after her marriage with the Russian Count Anatole Demidoff, her charms faded and her countenance wore an intrepid air of dissipation, not by any means uncommon in Frenchwomen of fashion.

The voyage to Brazil proved extremely agreeable. He passed the line, and was exempted by the politeness of the captain from the necessity of going through those ridiculous ceremonies which are still suffered to disgrace the navies of most civilised nations. Not being addicted to idleness he made good use of the captain's library, and read over again the works of Châteaubriand and Rousseau, together probably with many other books. But life on board ship is not favourable to study. The movement of the vessel, the shouting of the sailors, the troublesome routine interfere with the operations of the mind.

He has always studied in his letters as well as in his books, to introduce as frequently as possible passages calculated to awaken in the French mind ideas associated with Napoleon. In describing his voyage to Rio, he does not say the ship was impelled by an easterly wind, but by a wind from St. Helena. Towards this historic rock, in the depth of his emotions, he turned his eyes, but in vain. It would not appear, in fact it was much too far off, and no one, perhaps, but himself would have thought of alluding to it at all.

Descriptions of sea voyages are almost unavoidably monotonous, and perhaps therefore Louis Napoleon did well not to enlarge upon his naval experience. On New Year's Day, which the French keep with much greater solemnity than we do, all the officers entered his cabin to wish him a happy New Year. He drank, he says, his mother's health at dinner, and doubted not that at the same moment she was dining at Arenenberg, and forming similar fond wishes for him.   In the portion of his letter written on that day, he names a long list of friends, and begs to be remembered kindly to them all.

Four days afterwards, the frigate found itself in the midst of one of those tornadoes which vex the tropical portion of the Atlantic.   The English ride through storms and hurricanes like lords of the elements, and almost appear to believe in the existence of no danger on their native sea. It is different with our neighbours; they never take kindly to the ocean, and through their very dislike and antipathy greatly multiply the perils they encounter.   On the present occasion, one of the frigate's masts was blown away, while her sails were torn to ribands; a fortunate circumstance, as she might otherwise have capsised.   The rain fell in torrents, and covered the surface of the deep with white foam.   Louis Napoleon does not say so, but he probably then thought his last hour was come. Tropical storms, however, are not of long continuance.   The wind blew, the firmament was cleared of clouds, and a rich golden sunshine streamed down upon the waves.

In the course of a few days, the frigate arrived at Rio, the grand approaches to which made a strong impression on his mind. Previously to his leaving Europe, his mother, it seems, had expressed her intention of joining him in the New World. But from this he now dissuaded her. Do not come to me, he says, as I know not where I shall set up my abode, whether in the United States, or here in the south; but wherever I am, I must toil to earn my bread, which will be some consolation, as it will carry away my ideas from the painful subjects around which they might otherwise cluster.

The American packet having traversed the Atlantic more rapidly than the French frigate, he learned immediately on his arrival that his accomplices at Strasbourg had been put upon their trial and acquitted. In whatever light viewed, the conduct of the French Government throughout the whole of this affair was disreputable in the extreme. With the most profound contempt for justice, as well as for public opinion, it merely condemned the ringleader to a pleasant voyage across the Atlantic, in a ship of war, and at the public expense, while the subordinates, whether dupes or accomplices, were tried for their lives. Impressed by the iniquity of the transaction, the jury indignantly acquitted the whole body of the accused.

Connected with this process, Louis Napoleon

relates an anecdote highly characteristic of Louis
Philippe's justice. Before leaving France, he had
entrusted to the procureur-général a letter for
Colonel Vaudrey, in which he had taken upon himself
the whole culpability of the Strasbourg expedition ;
but as it might have been of some service to the
prisoners, it was withheld. Upon which he exclaims,
" What infamy ! " It was infamous no doubt; but
since that time, France has witnessed numerous circumstances connected with the prosecution of political
offenders which posterity will acknowledge to have
been considerably more flagitious.

Louis Napoleon found at New York, two of his
cousins, Achille and Lucien Murat, one of whom had
been honoured with the rank of colonel in the
American army, while the other held a lucrative civil
appointment. These facts may be said to indicate
one of the great dangers to which the Republic of
the United States is exposed. To afford an asylum
for refugees of all nations is at once humane and
wise, because it procures for the State universal
respect and esteem; but it is highly impolitic to
bestow important offices in the army or in the civil
service upon adventurers from other countries, who
can entertain no respect for the institutions of the
Republic, no affection for the people, and in most

cases little or no attachment for liberty. Should times of trouble unhappily arise, these fugitives from the Old World, with their corrupt education and monarchical notions, would probably be among the foremost to promote discord and endanger the safety of the commonwealth.

England throws open her hospitable shores to all classes of exiles, aristocrats and democrats, Republicans and legitimists, but she very prudently abstains from entrusting to them any department of public business. All history, ancient and modern, is full of the evils which exiles have brought upon communities, no less upon those in which they found refuge than upon their own. The former they have engaged, through the force of noble sympathies, in disastrous enterprises, while they have nearly always, when permitted to return to their homes, brought back along with them an accumulation of fierce and vindictive passions which have led to usurpations, revenge, persecution, and blood. The fact may be lamented in the interest of humanity, but a fact it is, and nations should endeavour at least to convert it into a lesson.

CHAP IX.

DEATH OF HORTENSE. THE SWISS IN ARMS.

LOUIS NAPOLEON did not remain very long in America, for his mother having written to say she was about to undergo a dangerous operation which might prove fatal, and expressing a wish to see him before her death, he set the government of Louis Philippe at defiance, once more traversed the Atlantic, and arrived at the Château of Arenenberg in time to close his mother's eyes, and receive her last blessing. Her remains were shortly afterwards conveyed to France and interred beside those of her mother in the church of Ruel near Malmaison, where her son, during his imprisonment at Ham, caused a monument with a dutiful and affectionate inscription to be erected to her memory.

Whatever may be thought of Louis Napoleon in the other relations of private or public life, he always appears to have behaved with singular dutifulness and affection towards his mother, who on her part was such a mother as is not often seen. In the course of the preceding narrative it must have appeared that she frequently risked her life in order to watch over his, while her thoughts were constantly employed in the endeavour to promote his welfare. This maternal affection awakened in him a corresponding feeling. From the earliest childhood he looked up to her with reverence, and through life preserved the most tender attachment for her.

They who are opposed to him on political grounds need not grudge him this praise. To have been nurtured in noble principles, to have acquired high notions of justice, truth and generosity, is to have impressed on our minds the great cardinal Christian virtue of doing to others what we would they should do to us; and therefore republican writers should be above all others careful to give every man his due. It is very certain that even tyranny itself is not always able to quench the feelings of the heart. A man rendered cruel by ambition towards a whole community, may nevertheless be susceptible of filial piety towards his father or his mother. At any rate Louis Napoleon appears to have been always a good son, gentle, tender, and affectionate in the highest degree; and if ever mother was calculated to inspire these feelings in a brave and true son it was Hortense.

Whether or not she was gay and giddy in her youth, it is not my business to inquire. Great good fortune often betrays women as well as men into the excesses of frivolity, but the first touch of misfortune brought out all the great qualities of Louis Napoleon's mother, and rendered her during the remainder of her life an example for high minded women to imitate. Few of her sex have experienced greater reverses, or supported them with more heroic courage. It is no slight distinction to be descended from such a mother. Wherever she went, admiration, respect, and love clustered about her: she formed in Switzerland the centre of a wide circle of beneficence, and to her virtue probably was due much of the influence exerted by Louis Napoleon over the government of the Cantons. Altogether there are few dwellings in Switzerland which deserve to be visited with greater reverence than that of Hortense Fanny Beauharnais, who lost much, and perhaps gained nothing, by having her name connected with the Bonaparte family.

No doubt the name of Napoleon procured for Louis Bonaparte a degree of consideration which would not otherwise have been shown him. He possessed much ability, but many others who equalled or surpassed him in this respect were far from sharing the same rewards, or commanding the same attention. The supreme government of Switzerland, as a mark of respect for imaginary services, honoured him with the rights of citizenship, and gave him a command in the Swiss army, which, however, was merely nominal, because in time of peace Switzerland maintains no standing forces. But his residence in the territories of the Republic was destined to bring upon the country no small inconvenience, and to expose it to no little danger. Louis Philippe, whose repose had already been disturbed by the expedition to Strasbourg, was very little inclined to look on quietly while preparations were making for a renewal of the attempt.

Regarding things from a philosophical point of view, it appears to me that both these men were right, or else that both were wrong. Louis Philippe was in possession of a throne which he had acquired by intrigue, and upon which he had no just claim whatever; he was therefore a pretender in possession, a fortunate usurper, a tyrant who had gained his point. But if we allow any force to the law of self-preservation, we must admit that, finding himself where he was, he was justified in endeavouring to remain there. Louis Napoleon, on the other hand, ambitious, restless, and intriguing also, thought he had as good a right as Louis Philippe to be the ruler of France, provided he could cajole the people into the same way of thinking.

I am amazed that authors not otherwise destitute of abilities, should yet, in writing the life of Louis Napoleon, be so weak as to descant like astrologers of the middle ages about stars, destiny, secret voices, and the religion of a man's blood. While reading their productions one appears to be listening to a number of ancient crones crowding around a country fire, and gossiping about fate and witchcraft. Old Napoleon had won numerous battles, defeated numerous kings and emperors, defrauded a great nation of its liberties, and raised himself to an imperial throne, only to be hurled down from it, and sent to expiate his ambition and his crimes on a solitary rock in the Atlantic.

When this great act of justice had been accomplished, the powers of Europe by whom it had been achieved should have paused before they took the next step. Had they been wise, they would have left France free to choose her own form of government, in which case it can hardly be doubted the nation would have established a Republic. This would have quenched for ever the Napoleonic idea, which is only another name for insatiable ambition.

Had the Republic succeeded, the peace of Europe
would have been preserved, for Republics are pacific
governments; had it failed, France might still have
had recourse to a limited monarchy, with a parliament
and free press, like that which was introduced by
the Revolution of July. But by going back to
the eighteenth century, taking out of its repository
two political mummies like Louis XVIII. and
Charles X., and forcing them down the throats of
the French nation with bayonets, they entailed upon
the country a series of shocks and changes, and made
people desire, in the misery and the humiliation of
the present, to return to the excitement, energy, and
glory of the past.

It was upon this sentiment, which the influence
of foreigners had fostered in the French, that Louis
Napoleon relied. What he aimed at was a fresh
restoration. The Bourbons had been restored, why
not the Bonapartes? Such was the state of things
after the return of Louis Napoleon from America
to Switzerland. If he did not plot, no doubt can
be entertained it was merely for want of the
means, not of the will. But though his will was
strong, his means were few, and had he been left
quietly where he was he might probably have
worn out his life in petty and fruitless machina-

tions. But Louis Philippe, whom, nevertheless, the world still calls wise, determined to confer on Louis Napoleon an European celebrity, vast importance in his own eyes and in the eyes of the Napoleonist party throughout France, and at the same time to invest him with the interest of a political martyr.

This was precisely the worst thing he could have done; but he did it, prudent old man that he was! He ordered his ambassador at Berne, the pompous and hollow-headed Montebello, to demand what the age had invented a new word to express — the extradition of Louis Napoleon. Expulsion might have done as well, but the world must have its novelties in language as in other things. The heart of Louis Napoleon swelled with joy at this foolish demand of the French Government. He felt that his fortune was made, and saw for the first time distinctly the star of empire twinkle in the remote distance. The cunning old man of the Tuileries had overreached himself. Up to this moment Louis Napoleon had been an adventurer, endeavouring, like Lambert Simnel or Perkin Warbeck, to do something for himself, but now he was elevated into the political opponent of the French king.

From this time forward, he played his cards with

superior dexterity. The secret voice of the Tuileries had proved itself to be less clever than the secret voice of Arenenberg. In the war of secret voices therefore, he had clearly the best of it, whatever the world might think to the contrary. The Swiss nation has by fits exhibited an immense amount of public spirit. It was in the humour to do so now, and therefore replied to the menaces of Montebello by evoking the ancient spirit of William Tell, and calling the citizens to arms. All its vallies flashed with bayonets and sabres; the gorges of the Alps bristled with cannon, and the few but daring Republicans determined again to adorn the borders of their lakes with pyramids of French bones. The cry of a second Morat, resounded from rock to rock, and the nerves of all men were strung for a prolonged and deadly struggle.

On the other hand, the French Government put its splendid battalions in motion — the tramp of foot and horse, the dull roll of gun carriages, the beating of drums, the loud notes of bugles and clarions rolled in one immense torrent towards the Alps.

CHAP. X.

THE SCENE CHANGES TO LONDON.

AT this moment, the voluntary act of an individual put a sudden stop to this vast dramatic exhibition, which might otherwise have stained half Europe with blood. Louis Napoleon having gained all he wanted—immense notoriety—quitted Switzerland, and came directly to London; upon which the storm ceased. The Genevese returned to the making of watches, the chamois hunters betook themselves to their old haunts in the upper Alps, the husbandmen laid aside the sword and the musket for the plough, and everything in the confederated cantons resumed its accustomed course.

Louis Philippe recalled his armies, and imagined he had gained a victory. He had only converted an insignificant enemy into a formidable one. But why did not the wise old man pursue the fugitive a little further? Why was not Duc de Montebello sent over to bluster and threaten in London? The right was the same. The only difference was, that the

Swiss were weak, and therefore, as Louis Philippe supposed, to be insulted with impunity, whereas the English were strong, and therefore not to be molested.

This is the part of Louis Napoleon's career upon which it is least pleasant to dwell. His star, his secret voice, his faith, the religion of his blood, were forgotten amid the too powerful charms of pleasure. But it is not my business to collect or publish scandalous anecdotes, and I leave it to those who may find the task congenial.

I believe his life was not what it ought to have been, but even if so, I do not care to inquire into it. If he gambled in London, or betted at Newmarket, or did other things still less to his credit, I make no doubt he felt the usual amount of remorse. Nemesis never dies, never sleeps, never withdraws her eyes for a moment from the career of man, to reward him for his virtues or punish him for his crimes. I only allude to this part of the subject to shame those literary sycophants who crawl at the footstool of power, and labour to elevate success into a divinity.

In the summer of 1840, Lord Eglinton amused and delighted the public by the revival of one of the magnificent exhibitions of the middle ages. He gave a grand tournament at his castle, in Scotland, to which Louis Napoleon was invited, and where he is said to have figured to advantage, even among the splendid nobility of England, by the tastefulness of his dress and the costliness of his appointments. The queen of beauty on the occasion was Lady Seymour, and the admiration of the guests was divided between her and the glorious scenery for which that portion of our island is remarkable. Even Louis Napoleon's eye, accustomed to the features of the Alps, must have dwelt with pleasure on the glens and forests and hills of Ayr.

Louis Napoleon's excesses and embarrassments, however, may have contributed to his material good fortune. The history of mankind supplies us with other and far greater examples. Cæsar overthrew the Roman Republic because he couldn't pay his debts, which many will allow to have been a legitimate cause, and Louis Napoleon made his descent on Boulogne for the same reason. He borrowed of all his friends, he took up money in London at extravagant interest, he connected himself with stock-jobbers, and having by such means raised the necessary sum, prepared once more to disturb the old man of the Tuileries in his enjoyment of regal state.

On this occasion, Louis Napoleon collected together

in London as many disaffected Frenchmen as were willing to hazard their heads for the chance of recovering their position in their own country. Yet the number was not great; since they amounted altogether to less than sixty. It has been stated, but this is not credible, that they were ignorant of the design in which they were engaged. They carried along with them a wooden eagle, freshly gilt, and a tame living eagle, which was intended to fly to the top of Napoleon's column. But though the French are much given to the worship of eagles, it was rather too much to expect that a whole nation should be roused to insurrection by beholding one of its fetishes on the top of a pillar.

This, therefore, may be regarded as the weak part of Louis Napoleon's scheme, though I am thoroughly convinced, that had his attempt succeeded, most of the writers who now throw ridicule on the idea would have considered it sublime. In fact, success is the only thing which makes divinities in the eyes of the vulgar. Had the *coup d'état* failed, the same writers would have denounced Louis Napoleon as a sanguinary miscreant, whereas, because it succeeded, they look upon him as a hero, and employ their servile pens in accomplishing his apotheosis. He no doubt regards with equal contempt their present praise and

former ridicule, seeing that both proceed from th
littleness and baseness of their minds.

Mankind have not yet become so paralysed by civi
lisation as not to sympathise with adventurous enter
prises. Everybody must acknowledge the darin;
courage which prompted a handful of men to procee(
in a hired steamer, to attempt the overthrow of a stron;
government and the subjugation of a large country
As the "City of Edinburgh" steamed down th(
Thames, and traversed the British Channel, th(
hearts of the Paladin conspirators must have beei
agitated by many conflicting feelings. Somewha
to calm the nerves of his associates, and to inspir(
them with momentary enthusiasm, he kept then
assembled round the social board, where the roas
beef was plentiful and the champagne flowed lik(
water. Yet neither beef nor champagne could
entirely still the beatings of their hearts as they
neared the French coast, upon which they wer(
about to land as enemies to the Government.

At length they did land, French chiefly, and Italians
and Louis Napoleon, like a knight errant, presented
himself to the officers on duty, and invited them to
abjure their allegiance to Louis Philippe, and accept
him for their emperor. But the souvenirs of the
empire were dying out in the army. A new gene-

ration of soldiers had arisen who knew not Napoleon, save by tradition, and these could hardly be expected to hazard or throw away their lives for a man whom they had never seen.

The conspirators rushed through the town, and ascended the heights to the foot of the column, shouting, " Vive l'Empereur." But the Picards proved unsusceptible, the eagle refused to soar to the summit of the column, the soldiers were immoveable. Nobody would pronounce in favour of this new Don Quixote. On the contrary, a number of officers advanced to arrest him and his companions, who, perceiving the failure of their enterprise, retreated towards the beach, and attempted to make their way through the waves to the steamer, which, faithful to its engagement, rode gallantly as nearly as possible to the shore for their reception.

Seeing the smallness of their numbers, the partisans of Louis Philippe became courageous, pursued them into the sea, and captured Louis Napoleon himself, who, drawing a pistol, and firing at his assailants, shot a grenadier. However, all at length were made prisoners, and forwarded to Paris for trial. M. de la Gueronnière, who has written an official panegyric on Louis Napoleon, is at a loss, with all his grandiloquence, upon what principle to defend the expedition to Boulogne. But it is defensible on various grounds. Regarding it as an invasion, of course the madness of the enterprise would exceed all description. But it was not contemplated by Louis Napoleon in that light. He believed, though as it proved erroneously, that the French army was eager to have once more a member of the Bonaparte family at its head, and that the French people generally shared the same sentiment. He therefore threw himself upon what he supposed to be a strong national feeling — he appealed to the prejudices of the French, to their military souvenirs, to what may almost be called their animal instincts. But the moment he selected was not propitious.

Louis Philippe had not yet filled up the measure of his iniquities, and people were content still to hope that a certain amount of liberty might be enjoyed under his profligate and avaricious sway. For this reason, Louis Napoleon failed in his undertaking. But no one who understands anything of the French people will pretend that his attempt was absurd, or extravagant, or hopeless. It was a mere chance that he did not succeed; and perhaps a little more previous arrangement, a more liberal distribution of five franc pieces, of beef sausages and champagne, would have completely answered his purpose, as it did afterwards on the plain of Satori.

Had his calculation been correct, Louis Philippe
would have been sent into exile eight years earlier
than he was, and the drama of the empire would
have commenced.   But through adverse circumstances Louis Napoleon's plan failed, and he proceeded under guard to Paris, to take the consequences.   He knew as well as any man in Europe,
that Louis Philippe's disposition was far from mild,
when the fate of persons who had made any attempt
against his life or his power was concerned.   A long
list of regicides had been already executed.   He stood
entrenched therefore within a circle of blood, and his
fears having been excited, it was not altogether certain that even Louis Napoleon's relationship to the
ex-emperor would protect him from the guillotine.

He himself however apprehended nothing of the
kind.   His former attempt had been punished
gently, by exportation in a French frigate to America.   With something similar Louis Philippe might
still be contented; but his mother Hortense was
dead, and he had therefore no eloquent intercessor
of that high influence to plead for him, and tyrants
generally grow fiercer as they advance in years.

After the Strasbourg affair, Louis Napoleon was
not brought to trial, but treated simply as a wild
youth, who required a little parental chastisement.

Circumstances were altered now. His case was brought before the Chamber of Peers, where he was arraigned and tried in due form. He selected as his defender the great legitimist lawyer, Berryer, who enjoyed an European reputation as much for his high honour and integrity as for his distinguished abilities as a pleader, a politician, and a statesman. M. Berryer undertook the task, and executed it in a masterly manner. His speech for the defence was remarkable for its logical acumen, and still more for its fervid appeals to the loftiest and noblest feelings of the heart as well as to the powers of the understanding. He did not hesitate to tell the judges home truths. He said, " Had M. Louis Napoleon succeeded, I can lay my hand upon my heart, and affirm most emphatically that I should not have profited in the slightest degree by his success. My feelings—my opinions—my principles— would have forbidden me. As many of you as can say the same are competent to be his judges, but none else. Not one should sit in judgment on him, who, had he accomplished his purpose, would have taken office under him and benefited by his power."

But his appeal was thrown away. The Chamber of Peers condemned Louis Napoleon to perpetual imprisonment, and he was soon removed from the

Conciergerie to the Château of Ham.   This castle, which is situated in the town of the same name, stands on the banks of the river Somme in Picardy, in the midst of dreary flats and marshes.   The walls of its lofty towers are thirty-six feet in thickness; it is surrounded by a wet ditch, and by ranges of inferior walls, with immense gates and drawbridges, so that the prisoner who happens to be confined there can experience but little hope of escape.   A man perched on the summit of the keep can command a view far and wide, over the moist level covered with aquatic plants and marsh flowers and intersected by the slow snake-like windings of the Somme.

PART THE THIRD.

~~~~~ ~

CHAPTER I.

THE CHÂTEAU OF HAM

CONSIDERING the character of the French Government in nearly all ages, it seems hardly too much
to suspect that Ham was chosen to be a state prison
as much for the malaria of the neighbourhood as for
the thickness of its walls. We know that in the
Papal States men of proud minds and enlightened
principles have been sent to acquire humility in the
pestilential dungeons of the Campagna, where their
dimmed eyes, yellow complexion and trembling
limbs, have avenged their attachment to liberty and
the Republic. By views such as these Louis
Philippe may have been guided in his choice of a
state prison. But some men, like certain other
animals, thrive in moist places. Louis Napoleon
felt more than his usual vivacity in the Château of
Ham, whose dull and sluggish atmosphere seems to

have brought comfort to his imagination. He passed quite naturally from English field-sports, *rouge-et-noir*, betting at Newmarket, and other civilised amusements, to the enjoyments of this pleasant solitude. He had a garden on the terrace in which he may possibly have cultivated pansies and forget-me-nots. He had another garden inaccessible to Louis Philippe and his myrmidons, in which he planted and trailed a different kind of flowers—ambition, intrigue, bitterness and revenge. Both these little plots were attended to with equal industry and equal gaiety, and he made some resolutions there which he has since kept.

An old friend of mine, M. Frederick de George, was at that time editor of the " Propagateur du Pas-de-Calais." He was, and probably still is, one of those amphibious entities, half republican, half Bonapartist, which were once common in France, though they are so no longer. With the journal of this very able man, Louis Napoleon maintained a correspondence, not constant, nor even frequent, but at intervals sufficiently short to keep his name from fading out of public view. He unquestionably did not believe that his imprisonment would be perpetual. It was matter of astonishment not only to him but to all the world, that any French

revolutionary government should have lasted so long
as that of Louis Philippe already had.

Having studied the law of political storms, he
came to the conclusion that one of them must soon
occur to blow open his prison doors, and indulge the
French people with a little wholesome change. He
therefore set himself cheerfully to work, studying
statistics, poor laws, organisation of labour, and such
like, not at all doubting the speedy advent of some
political tempest. He seems, however, not previously
to have made the discovery that French governments
may by chance last from fifteen to seventeen years.
That was about the period allotted by his star to
Napoleon; the Bourbons, after their restoration, remained in their mummy-like state above ground for
about the same period; and he should therefore have
concluded that Louis Philippe, by his superior cunning and adroitness, might defy the fates quite as
long as any of his predecessors.

The triumphs and public works of the old Napoleon, had generally created the belief, that all the
members of his family were equal to anything.
They themselves also shared this prevalent superstition; and in reality the spirit of the French revolution had inspired them with the belief that most
things in the world might be altered for the better;

that scarcely anything was impracticable; and that whatever could be accomplished by human force or ingenuity could be accomplished by them. Joseph during his reign at Naples, had constructed great roads over half the kingdom, and meditated the opening up of the canal between the Adriatic and Tyrrhene seas, originally projected by the Romans; Eugène Beauharnais had laid down a plan for deepening the channel and regulating the course of the Po; and Napoleon himself, after having flung stupendous roads across the Alps, resolved to convert Paris into a seaport.

These vast designs, though never fully realised, spread the fame of the Bonapartes even to the New World; and, in consequence, while Louis Napoleon lay a prisoner at Ham, a deputation from Central America waited upon him to propose that he should superintend the construction of the projected canal which was to unite the Atlantic and Pacific Oceans. On this point, however, there was some one else to be consulted. It was not for Louis Napoleon to decide whether he would undertake the mighty task or not. M. Louis Philippe had a potent voice in the matter, and he determined that the good people of Central America should organise their joint stock company and excavate their canal without the personal superintendence of his state prisoner. He made no objection, however, to his writing on the subject, and accordingly Louis Napoleon with great patience and ingenuity drew up a sort of prospectus for the Nicaraguan projectors, in which he demolished, at least to his own satisfaction, the pretensions of all the other routes across the isthmus. This pamphlet, which was not published till some time afterwards, may still be read with pleasure. The writer had studied the subject thoroughly, and threw so much earnestness into his little work, that although he does not always succeed in convincing the reader of the practicability of his scheme, he never fails to interest his imagination and excite the wish that the project might be realised.

Just before leaving England he had published a political work entitled " Napoleonic Ideas," which though since discovered to be something wonderful, attracted at the time very little notice.

But in the Château of Ham, he found some consolation in writing. He had an active mind, and though without depth of thought or originality, could always put what ideas he possessed into a neat and agreeable form. This is more praise than can be bestowed on most emperors who affect to be literary. Old Napoleon himself when he took up the pen

produced nothing but gorgeous bombast; and therefore it is no small praise for his nephew to say that
he can write agreeably, and that his letters are often
models of adroitness and policy. If ever man made
the most of himself it is Louis Napoleon. His abilities
are not great, but he has the judgment to estimate
them correctly, and to adapt them to the exgencies
of an age in which greatness is a tradition rather
than a contemporary reality. Louis Napoleon, with
much patience and skill, studied the French people,
their wants and their weaknesses, and then took into
consideration the number and extent of his own
faculties. Though his writings produced no great
effect, he still persevered, and cast his bread upon
the waters, not doubting that he should find it after
many days. He corresponded meanwhile with several persons, among others with Count D'Orsay and
Lady Blessington, who appeared to him a poetical
and high minded woman. Here in England, we
form a different appreciation of her; but there is no
accounting for tastes.

While in this prison Louis Napoleon, in one of
those letters which were so many manifestoes composed with immense care, expressly for circulation,
observed that he was in his place, for that he could
only exist in the gloom of a dungeon, or amid the

splendours of power.   Translated into plain English, this phrase only means, that he had grown extremely tired of Ham, and would rather be an emperor if he could.   The feeling was perfectly natural, and most persons in the same situation would have shared it with him.   The fascinations of the sugar question, and pauperism, and stoicism, and Lady Blessington were soon exhausted.

He became impatient of confinement as year after year passed, and no one presented himself to assassinate Louis Philippe or overthrow his government. What was to be done ?   He could no longer act the hero; the system of the Portico had become nauseous; he felt no solace in uttering or writing big sentences, in affecting not to feel what he did feel.   He became convinced that he was not in his place, and that Ham, although situated on the beloved soil of France, was far from being a pleasant residence.   No one had ever thought it so, and least of all Louis Napoleon himself.   I sympathise with him sincerely, and so would all those Republicans who now linger out their lives in the tropical morasses of Cayenne or amid the fiery deserts of Africa, if he would suffer them again to tread the French soil which they love as well as he.

But I anticipate.   France, by which he could now

R

understand nothing but the word Ham, became hateful to him, and he longed at all hazards to escape from it. To augment his strong desire for liberty, his father wrote to him from Florence saying that he was old, that his health, which had never been good, was now worse than ever, and that he wished to see his only son before his death. This supplied Louis Napoleon with a just and honourable reason for desiring to leave his prison, that he might go to comfort the ex-king of Holland on his death-bed in Tuscany. He wrote to Louis Philippe demanding permission to perform this filial office, and pledging himself in due time to return to his prison.

The crafty old king found himself placed in a situation of much perplexity. If he refused, he knew he should be denounced both by republicans and Bonapartists as a cruel and unnatural tyrant; if he consented, he should let loose an enemy whose exasperated vindictiveness he had the greatest possible reason to fear. Matters would not be greatly mended even should Louis Napoleon's policy induce him to return to his prison, because the credit for magnanimity which he would thereby gain might prove extremely injurious to the house of Orleans.

He took counsel of the spirit of Machiavelli, and having well deliberated on the matter, returned

through his ministers such an answer as Louis Napoleon might have expected. The generous monarch,
they said, respecting his filial piety, would not oppose
his journey to Florence; but out of consideration
for the peace of the country and the good of the
French people, things always uppermost in his mind,
he was constrained to insist on certain conditions,
agreeing to which would for ever have frustrated
the designs of Louis Napoleon.

That stoicism is tolerably tough which enables a
man for nearly six years to wear a close mask in
prison. But Louis Napoleon was not in possession
of this stern philosophy. He had in him nothing
of the ancient Roman. He affected to be calm,
but his words betrayed his agitation; he pretended
not to feel, but his letters revealed the anguish and
impatience of his mind. He read, he wrote, he
meditated; he planted flowers, he watched their
growth; he heard from the Count and Countess de
Montholon endless anecdotes of the exile of St.
Helena; he devoured novels, he corresponded with
their authors; but when in an honest mood, he confessed that these things filled up his time but not his
mind.

He panted to be at large. Yet he was far more
fortunate than most prisoners. There have been

persons who for want of human society have cultivated the partiality of a spider or a toad, and
taught those loathsome and repulsive creatures
to love and confide in them. They possessed
life, and therefore were interesting to men who
could associate with nothing else which enjoyed
that blessing.

Louis Napoleon had companions high and low,
and among others his physician and his valet.
Dr. Conneau had been the friend of his mother,
and through mere attachment to him had sought
and been permitted to share his prison. After
the refusal of the French Government to allow him
to visit his father, Louis Napoleon made up his
mind to effect his escape in defiance of it. He
held, therefore, with Dr. Conneau numerous mysterious conversations, the object of which was the
recovery of his liberty. Upon the means it was
difficult to decide. Soldiers, the invariable instruments of despotism, swarmed about the Château
of Ham, mixing familiarly with the jailers, and
differing from them in nothing but in name.

But there is much wisdom in the old English
saying, " Where there's a will there's a way." Nothing is impossible to energy, courage and resolution.
The doctor and the prince put their wits together,

and the result was a plan of escape, ingenious and novel, but attended with considerable risk. In the month of March 1846, that portion of the castle in which Louis Napoleon resided was thought to need repair, and a number of workmen were introduced for the purpose of effecting it. Now, therefore, was the time to try the value of their stratagem.

Louis Napoleon, affecting to be ill, kept his bed for two or three days, and was carefully watched over by his physician. This worthy descendant of Machaon had meantime turned his anatomical knowledge to account, and constructed a lay figure in size and appearance resembling his patient, and destined to play an important part in the drama to be forthwith enacted.

CHAP. II.

ESCAPE.—ANECDOTES.

ONE morning very early a workman's dress was procured and brought into the prison by one of the masons. It was soiled and limed, and considerably worn; a workman's hat, battered and slouching, covered the prisoner's head, and a pair of heavy *sabots* concealed his feet. When all was ready, the lay figure was placed in the imaginary sick man's bed; the sick man himself, strong and active, took up a large plank, and placed it sideways on his shoulder, so as partly to conceal his face. He glided out, and stood for a short time among the other workmen, then with a clownish gait passed on, descended the castle stairs through files of soldiers, passed the sentinel, traversed the spacious court, and approached the great arched gateway of the fortress, leading out over a drawbridge into the town. But there, unfortunately, stood an officer, and the prisoner felt that to escape his lynx eyes would be far more difficult than to baffle the scrutiny of labourers and sentinels.

But fortune is sometimes in good humour, even when least expected. The worthy officer was probably in love, and had just received a letter containing perhaps an assignation. He opened it, and stood reading while Louis Napoleon with the plank on his shoulder, and with increasing anxiety in his heart, drew near. Plunged in Elysian dreams, or agitated with rage by indications of perfidy, the officer never raised his eyes from the paper. Numerous workmen were passing in and out, and many of them turned an inquiring eye upon their would-be comrade, the features of whose countenance they could not recognise. Several stopped to look at him; the moment was critical; with as much *sangfroid* as he could command, he threw down the plank, and walked at an accelerated pace down the street.

Presently he had left the town, and in a shady lane close by leaped into a carriage which, by the contrivance of his worthy valet, had been stationed there to wait for him. He threw off his *sabots*, laid aside his blouse and his workman's hat, and with all practicable speed made his way towards St. Quentin and the Belgian frontier.

He had not, however, proceeded far on the road

before suspicion began to be excited in the prison.
When the time arrived for breakfast, Dr. Conneau
ordered it to be laid out in his room, observing
that the prince was ill, and would be agitated by
the entrance of the servants into his apartment.
The doctor said he would himself take him what
he needed. At the usual hour, the governor came
to pay his respects to the prince, but was informed
that having passed a very bad night, which was
no doubt true, he was now asleep, and that it would
be cruel to disturb him. With this reasonable
account the governor was satisfied, and went quietly
away.

By and by, however, in due course of time, he presented himself again, and was met with the same
story. He now, however, became a little more in-
quisitive, and insisted upon seeing his prisoner. The
doctor took him into the room, and pointed to the bed
on which he lay asleep: the governor was once more
satisfied. Towards evening the man in authority
came a third time, but when the doctor gravely represented his patient as still under the influence of
his narcotic, the governor began to fear he had
taken under his charge one of the seven sleepers
of Ephesus.

He determined this time to rouse the slumberer.

Dr. Conneau had hoped to postpone the discovery
till the following morning, by which Louis Napoleon, if undetected, might be beyond the frontier.
But his ingenuity was exhausted. The governor
would hear no excuse, he advanced towards the bed,
he put forth his hand, he gently shook the supposed
sleeper. He was petrified with astonishment and
dismay. Turning to the Doctor, he inquired, more
in apprehension than in anger, " At what hour did
the prince escape ? " " At seven o'clock this morning," replied Dr. Conneau.

The alarm was instantly given ; the *gendarmes,*
the *chasseurs* scoured the country in all directions.
Everybody dreaded the anger of Louis Philippe,
and panted for the five franc pieces which would
no doubt be showered liberally on the fortunate
captor. But Louis Napoleon had so much the
start of them, that they galloped, shouted, and
swore in vain. He reached the frontier, he passed
into Belgium, and was soon merrily on his way to
London.

On arriving in town, he drove down immediately to Gore House to see Count D'Orsay. That
individual, as is well known, stood in rather hostile
relationship to certain tradesmen in London, who
occasionally, by their agents, became rather trouble-

some. When therefore it was announced to him, that a man of somewhat sinister aspect was in the hall, who desired to speak with him, but refused to give his name, the count in apprehension sent back the servant to say that unless he would explain who he was, he must go away, for he could not see him. Louis Napoleon, having probably some suspicion of the true state of the Count's mind, soon began to see the point of the joke, and determined to keep alive his friend's fears. He therefore sent back the servant saying, " Tell your master that I have come on business ; that I positively must see him, and will not go away until I do." " What does he look like ? " inquired the Count. " Something like a foreigner," said the man, " with an odd looking mouth and very big mustachios." " It is Louis Napoleon ! " exclaimed D'Orsay, and rushing out went and embraced him in the lobby. ·

During his stay in London, Louis Napoleon accompanied a lady of rank to the neighbourhood of Windsor. We have arrived at that period in the development of civilisation, in which, as in old age, it is more customary to look backwards than forwards. We love to recall the past, we almost dread to face the ominous future. Louis Napoleon has in his nature nothing whatever of this weakness. He scorns equally the past and the future, and lives entirely in the present. The lady misunderstood him, and imagining he would share her dreamy political sentimentality, whether real or affected, took him to the forest, of which she related the following circumstance. Immediately after the execution of Charles I., by the order of no one knew whom, the summits of all the grand trees were cut off, that they might appear to share the fate of their king. But in order to prefigure the restoration, nature immediately undid the work of the destroyer, forcing up her abundant and prolific sap through the trunks until the trees again shot forth new heads and new branches far more luxuriant and magnificent than those which had been cut away.

Louis Napoleon admired the forest, but experienced no emotion at the story, and on their way to London rallied his friend on her poetical enthusiasm. He cared no more for Charles or his head than for the last breakfast of king Pharamond. I have heard many anecdotes of Louis Napoleon during this period of his life, but as they are most of them discreditable, and may be apocryphal, I forbear to relate them. He was admitted, no doubt, into good society, but his habitual associates were at once inferior in taste and rank. He saw in the English aristocracy no element with which he could work. Too proud and listless to meddle with foreign intrigue; too opulent to be tempted by the chances of gain; too full of honour and fidelity to compromise the interests of their country, by actively favouring usurpation or change of dynasties in a neighbouring state, they received Louis Napoleon at their tables, but refused to participate in any of his schemes of revolution.

Whatever may now be pretended, he himself began to despair of discovering any opening by which he might make his way to power in France. The jargon about his star, about his secret voice, about his mysterious impulses, about the religion of his blood, gradually sank more and more out of sight. He affected less mysticism and more common sense. There exists in the English very little aptitude to be influenced by enthusiasm. We are a jolly, practical, and rather calculating people, and they among us are clearly the exceptions who suffer themselves to be carried away in real life by the fictions of the imagination. Perhaps we infuse too little poetry into our daily life, but the absence of this propensity at least enables us to steer very wide of those fantastic hallucinations, which, for

more than a century, have plunged the French
people into extravagant and useless experiments in
politics; into dreamy, unintelligible, unspiritual speculations in philosophy; into a fantastical, gauzy,
unnatural style in literature. Louis Napoleon has
in his nature a large infusion of the English character, but greatly prefers having Frenchmen to
work with. He very easily, however, made himself
at home in England, and having no other employment for his mind, betook himself, as in all former
periods of his life, to the mingled excitement of pleasure and study.

In this way, he passed his time, till the revolution of 1848 once more awakened his hopes.
The circumstances of Louis Philippe's downfal
have been too often described to render it necessary for me to dilate upon them. La Guer-
ronnière describes, with vindictive delight, the old
man of the Tuileries sneaking into a hackney coach
on the Place de la Révolution, and making his way
as best he could towards the English coast. He
had deserved his fate, and came here to die in
neglect and obscurity. Upon hearing of his fall,
Louis Napoleon went to his cousin, Lady Douglas,
and observed, "In less than a year from this time,
I shall be at the head of the French Government."

His partisans affect to regard this in the light of a prediction, which was fulfilled on the 10th of December.   He had, however, uttered similar words in 1836 and 1840, but the miscarriages of Strasburg and Boulogne overthrew his claims to be regarded as a prophet.

When there is a revolution in France, there is generally a subordinate movement in England.   The chartists were rendered vivacious by the events of February, and sought in the old jog trot way to promote their own favourite reforms — five or six points or more, by assembling in the open air, hearing bad speeches, and drawing up interminable petitions to parliament.   A great majority of them never had the least idea of fighting.   They had not been brought up to it, and did not know how to fight.   There were moral chartists, and physical force chartists, but neither the one nor the other had any great or particular significance.   Still the English Government felt uncomfortable, and observing great gatherings here and there about the metropolis—in Trafalgar Square, for example, and on Kennington Common—thought it necessary to make a demonstration to prevent the Five Points men from imitating the military population of Paris.

On the tenth of April, it should have been the

first, there was a great deal of noise on the other side of the water, and several timid people of both sexes urged the authorities to take precautions against the poor harmless multitude, which meant nothing in the world beyond exercising its ears and lungs in the fine open air of the southern suburbs.

We have a peculiar way of doing business here in London.   Silly people talked of cavalry and artillery, but ministers very wisely restricted their precautions to swearing in an immense number of special constables, among whom Louis Napoleon took his place.   He was always an active citizen, no matter whether he had any right or not.   In Paris a member of my family nearly lost his head by joining the mob against Louis Philippe.   The French dislike the interference of foreigners, and in my opinion very properly.   But if Englishmen have no right to figure in French insurrections, Louis Napoleon had quite as little to enlist among the opponents of the chartists.   He knew nothing of the Five Points, except what he had learned from the babble of Gore House, where a few dawdling aristocrats, without political or social standing, congregated to discuss the affairs of the empire.

From this petty exhibition however of vain and vulgar intermeddling, he was soon to be called to play

an important part in a far greater drama. It would
be harsh and ungenerous to maintain that the French
are incapable of freedom, though all the attempts
they have hitherto made to emancipate themselves
have been very ill managed. They imagine they
have some way of their own to establish liberty, and
despise at once the teachings of history and the
suggestions of contemporary experience. They may
emerge from this vicious dream, and organise a free
government hereafter ; but what I have known and
seen of them inspires me with strong apprehensions.
Still it is impossible to deny that they have made
prodigious sacrifices for liberty ; that whether they
have understood it rightly or not, they have argued
for it, fought for it, bled for it, with a courage and
disinterestedness almost unexampled in modern
times.

It may be, therefore, that Providence will
still, in its own good time, reward them with the
immense blessing which they have so long coveted.
They have every honest man's best wishes, and here
in England there are millions who would experience
great personal satisfaction at beholding a free constitution, whether republican or semi-monarchical,
like our own, established among our intelligent and
gallant neighbours. But the history of what the
French did in 1848 is calculated to cast a damp over

the spirits of every friend of liberty. Among the individuals who sought to establish the Republic, there
was scarcely a single statesman. Poets, orators, journalists, filled with the traditions of 1793, profoundly
versed in the affairs of Utopia, brimful of philanthropy, violent in the hatred of their aristocracy,
equally violent in their worship of the people, they
were eager to establish a degree of liberty more per·
fect than the world had ever witnessed. Every man,
like the Abbé Sièyes, went about with twenty new
constitutions in his pocket. The world was to be
turned upside down. In the civic raptures of some
persons the coming of a time was predicted in which
everybody was to command, and nobody to obey —
in which there would be no taxes, no armies, no magistrates, no anything. The old visions of Lubber-
land were to be realised. Lambs ready roasted and
vegetables ready cooked were to run about the
streets, crying, Come eat me. It required no profound sagacity to foresee that such a state of
things would prove of short duration

The insurrection of June broke out, and in order
to see how the French managed those matters, I
took a passport, and went over to Paris. All
France was in an uproar. In the towns along the
sea-coast, the people were overwhelmed with terror,

the railways were partially stopped. At the Boulogne station a few travellers assembled in the grey of the morning, and exerted all their eloquence to get a train started. They were answered by frightful stories about the taking up of the rails, the burning of stations, the planting of artillery along the line to blow out the steam trains into infinite space. After two or three hours' delay, a train did start in spite of all those frightful anticipations and predictions. At Amiens something of the grim reality presented itself. A train came in from Paris, bearing the remains of some few of those who had fallen in attempting to storm the barricades. I saw a father frantic with grief, bringing home the body of his only son, and then hiding himself that he might not face the first burst of the mother's agony. Everything was gloom, mourning, death-like.

Our train went on, and as we approached Paris passed between stations black and charred with flames; the rails had been loosened, or rather taken away and replaced, the engine moved slowly, the cannons still boomed in the distance, the train paused again and again, and it was not until near midnight that we reached the capital, where we ought to have arrived early in the afternoon. The roar of artillery had ceased, but fear still hung over everything. There were no hackney coaches, no cabs, very few people on the platform. It seemed probable we should have to pass the night at the station, as no persons were permitted to traverse the streets on foot. At length a carriage was procured, and we descended into the city. The streets were silent, solitary, deserted, yet all the houses were lighted up as if by invisible hands. Here and there soldiers standing still with fixed bayonets and loaded muskets, cried out to each other, as our vehicle moved slowly along, " *Sentinel, prenez garde à vous.*" Several times our carriage was stopped and examined in the supposition that we might be carrying ammunition to the insurgents.

As we drew near the Place de la Révolution, the loud roar of musketry was heard in the Tuileries gardens. We stopped and inquired what that meant, but were desired to drive on, and ask no questions. What the truth may have been I know not, but the sentinel placed at the door of the house we entered assured us in a whisper that they were shooting the insurgents whom they had taken prisoners; four hundred and thirty, as we were afterwards told. Certain it is, that a large square pit had been dug in the gravel, and that the public were excluded for a fortnight until the tramp of soldiers had levelled the path. Next morning I went out. Along the Boulevards the soldiers were bivouacked as in the open field, with their tents, their camp-fires, their stacks of musketry, and here and there a piece of artillery with cannonniers standing behind it, matches lighted, and faces covered with blood and dust.

The Place de la Révolution had been transformed into a camp for cavalry and artillery. Fires were blazing, horsemen riding to and fro. Heavy guns moved occasionally along the pavement. In several places stood the mortars which had thrown shells into the Faubourg St. Lazare still black with powder. Pyramids of round shot were piled up in streets, and in the open spaces before the palaces, the public offices and the Parliament House. In the disturbed quarters, vast barricades, constructed with paving stones, rose above the first floor windows. Pools of blood lay half dried in the streets. Houses riddled with cannon balls tottered, and threatened to fall upon the passengers; and enormous crowds, many dressed in mourning for those who fell in February, others wearing the marks of more recent grief upon their faces, moved gloomily along the thoroughfares. The shops still remained shut, and everything appeared to betoken the entire breaking up of society.

When the tumult of men's minds had somewhat subsided I went out in the evening, and met at parties nearly all the members of the Provisional Government. What they may have been in the Council, or in the Bureaux, I am unable to say; but in conversation they exhibited very little political wisdom. There was agitation, effervescence, declamation, wild hopes, fierce antipathies, but nothing like settled political convictions. Almost everybody reverted to the events of the Great Revolution, and seemed desirous of re-enacting the scenes of 1793.

The men who stood foremost at that epoch are well known to the world: Cavaignac, Ledru-Rollin, Lamartine, Armand Marrast, Louis Blanc, the Abbé Lamennais, Victor Hugo. It is difficult to draw the portraits of contemporaries, because the whole life not being before us, they may, even while we write, abjure their former principles, develope new traits of character, and become, in short, the very antipodes of what they appeared to be at first. But we can only draw what we see. If men change after we have delineated them, that is no fault of ours. Future history can take them up where we lay them down, and do ample justice to their metamorphoses.

CHAP. III.

FOUNDERS OF THE REPUBLIC.

IN order properly to estimate the intellectual power exhibited by Louis Napoleon, it seems necessary to appreciate those to whom, in 1848, he was opposed in the attempt to gain the suffrages of the French people. Among the chief of these was Lamartine, who stood for a while at the head of the Provisional Government. In considering the career and weighing the merits of this man, many persons have entered upon the fruitless discussion as to whether an author be or be nót calculated to prove a man of business. Authors, like other men, differ very much from each other. While some, therefore, are capable of turning their attention to politics, and of distinguishing themselves in the government of mankind, others fail altogether in the attempt. It might have been foreseen from the beginning that Lamartine would never prove a practical public man, not because he wrote poetry, or novels, or romantic histories, but because he was

destitute of firm and consistent political principles.
Nature may be said to have composed him of
jarring elements—his father having been a legitimist and his mother an Orleanist. He was consequently brought up and nurtured in hostile traditions, verging sometimes towards the one side,
sometimes towards the other. This was an extremely bad preparation for political and moral
consistency. He did not when a boy know what he
was, or what he ought to be, and throughout his
whole youth and manhood he perpetually fluctuated
between contending theories. He began life as a
Bourbonist, and throve by the patronage of Charles X.

After the Revolution of July, he ranked among the
supporters of Louis Philippe, but as that monarch's
calculating tactics and dynastic despotism developed
themselves, Lamartine went over to the opposition,
and cooperated assiduously with those who brought
about the Revolution of February. He then rose
suddenly to temporary power and influence, and
had he possessed the qualities of a statesman might
have played a distinguished part in public life.

But he was in fact perplexed by fantastic theories,
and blindly cooperated with those who, instead of
contenting themselves with establishing freedom,
desired to reconstruct the whole edifice of society

That there are evils and imperfections in the
manners, habits, and domestic institutions of modern
nations, it is impossible to deny; but they may
perhaps be incurable. At all events the authors of
the social theories at that time prevalent in France,
had put forward no new scheme of things which
would bear the test of philosophical analysis.
Lamartine, however, was carried away by the new
ideas. At first Louis Napoleon, who in principle
was also a socialist, appears to have stood in awe of
Lamartine's eloquence, which swayed not only the
National Assembly but the vast turbulent menacing
population of Paris.

Standing on the steps of the Hotel-de-Ville,
with the waves of an angry multitude surging
up fiercely towards him, the orator waved them
proudly back, and sending forth · his sonorous
and practised voice among them, excited their
curiosity, riveted their attention, and stilled their
passions. In parliamentary warfare, however, mere
impassioned speaking is not enough. They who
undertake to make laws for a great people look
more for breadth of thought, steadiness of views,
and stability of personal character, than for an
artificial rhetoric and poetical figures of speech.

Louis Napoleon soon discovered Lamartine's
weak side, and ceased to fear his opposition. By a

few plain strong words, implying in the speaker
an iron will and indomitable courage, he totally
neutralised the effect of Lamartine's rhetoric. When
he rose in the National Assembly, he greatly
reminded all historical students of the first appearance of Cromwell in the British Parliament; not
that there was an exact resemblance, but that both
possessed that peculiar quality which, when a man
speaks, rivets the attention of his listeners, partly
through apprehension, partly through the desire to
penetrate the dark problem of his character. From
the day on which Louis Napoleon was elected
President of the Republic, Lamartine's reputation
began to wax pale and dim, and he soon degenerated
into a partisan and an adulator, which he still con-
tinues to be.

Victor Hugo differs in many respects from Lamartine, though his origin and education were in a
great measure similar. He also has been everything
by turns, and nothing long; but since the *coup
d'état*, he has been content to cast his bread upon the
waters of liberty, to throw in his lot with the
fiercest and most resolute exiles, and to await in
hope and confidence the reappearance of that Don
Sebastian of the French people, a democratic Republic.
Of course Victor Hugo was in no sense the rival,

though he was among the enemies of Louis Napoleon. He had no traditions to oppose to the traditions of the Empire. In literary genius, he is as much superior to Louis Napoleon, as he is inferior to him in the art of interesting and ruling the mind of a vain people. His works are familiar to all Europe. Though exaggerated and fantastic, they are so replete with genius, that they awaken a powerful interest in the mind of every reader. Whatever he touches, he vivifies. Subjects the most unpleasant become tolerable in his hands; he creates a place for the most grotesque characters in our memory; he abounds in touches of true pathos, in striking contrasts, in rich colouring, in vivid and impetuous narrative. Nevertheless, Louis Napoleon might, I think, permit him to return to France with safety, for it is not in politics that his strength lies. His world is the world of the imagination, in which he is great, not the steady, sober, every-day world, over which it is impossible he should exercise any powerful or permanent influence.

The Abbé Lamennais, a man of rare genius and prodigious powers of intellect, was opposed to Louis Napoleon upon peculiar grounds. His antecedents had been strangely varied. Born in the bosom of the Catholic Church, he had emancipated himself from all its prejudices, and become in the truest sense of the word a Protestant. He was at the same time a socialist in politics, a hater of monarchy, an enemy to the privileged classes, a Jacobin, a leveller, a French Jack Cade. With the enthusiasm of a martyr, and the manners of a saint, he exposed himself to all kinds of persecution for the sake of a people who therefore loved him with extraordinary affection. He was the apostle and oracle of the Faubourg St. Antoine, during and after the insurrection of June; those fierce combatants for liberty repaired to his lodgings, as to a Delphian cavern, for inspiration, so that you could hardly ascend or descend his stairs in the Rue Châteaubriand without meeting some workman, or some workman's wife, who had consulted, or was coming to consult, the friend and prophet of their class.

But the Abbé's ambition was internal. He never coveted power or authority, never sought honours in the church or in the state. If he became a member of the French Parliament, it was that he might act there as the organ of the working classes, and see, as far as in him lay, that something like justice was done to them. His political theory was essentially opposed to that of the empire, and his light went out in the attempt to guide the Parisians towards freedom.

There were many other individuals at that time in
Paris, who, by their writings or their eloquence,
might advance or retard the designs of Louis Napoleon ; Proudhon, Louis Blanc, Armand Marrast,
together with a crowd of journalists, pamphleteers,
novel writers and metaphysicians. Of Proudhon's
character and career it is difficult to speak. His
genius has flashed forth from time to time in startling
paradoxes, sustained by extraordinary powers of
logic. Louis Blanc is paradoxical too, but in a
different way. He has derived his inspiration from
the eighteenth century, but clothes the ideas he puts
forward in an extremely modern dress. As books
exercise in France a much greater influence than
with us, Louis Blanc, by a systematic hostility to the
government of Louis Philippe, had at once greatly
damaged the Orleans dynasty, and augmented his
own reputation. But upon the establishment of the
Republic, having been elevated by circumstances
into an official situation, his remarkable abilities as a
writer only served to bring out into stronger relief
his deficiency in administrative talent. His written
page glows with vitality, his political conduct was
dreamy, languid, and vacillating.

Armand Marrast, with much less literary power,
had a greater aptitude for business ; but taken alto-

gether, the creators of the new Republic were inferior
to the situation in which they found themselves.   It
was their task to overthrow, not to build up.   From
the very commencement, therefore, it became clear to
careful observers that they must soon be driven off
the scene, to make way for men, inferior, perhaps, in
ability, but more accustomed to exercise that sort of
intelligence which is conversant with the management of affairs.

CHAP. IV.

RETURN OF THE BONAPARTES.

I NOW come to notice the cardinal error of the French people, the removal of the ostracism from the Bonaparte family. This act of folly was, moreover, perpetrated at the most inauspicious moment; when the capital and the whole country were in confusion; when a puerile enthusiasm pervaded a majority of the nation; when the upper orders were intoxicated with vanity and the multitude with false hopes and a maudlin generosity. Then, to increase the public disorder and to diminish immensely the chances of a favourable settlement of public affairs, the members of Napoleon's family, who had always been torches of discord, were permitted to return, and add their vanities and pretensions to the other causes, already too numerous, of public calamity.

They who look upon politics as a theme for school-boys, not as a subject to occupy and task to the utmost the mental powers of the greatest statesmen, declaimed about the injustice of excluding these worthy citizens from their country. They had yet to

be taught by experience that the highest justice is
that which prefers the good of the whole to the particular benefit of the few.   Nations do not exist for
each individual citizen, but each individual citizen
exists for the nation.   A good man and a great man,
capable of lofty attachment to his native land, would
prefer living and dying in exile, if he could thereby
promote the freedom and happiness of millions, to returning, with whimpering sentimentality, to maunder
about experiencing happiness in a French dungeon
rather than in the free atmosphere of England, or
amid the unbounded prairies and savannahs of the
New World.

But the members of the Bonaparte family are not
patriots.   Selfishness disguised under big words has
always been their principle of action.   Louis Napoleon especially had proved sufficiently before the
events of 1848 that he contemplated France and
the French people merely in the light of things
by which he might himself thrive.   The French
people, on the other hand, were poor spirited enough
to imagine that they could neither secure nor
enjoy their liberty without the presence of these
individuals.

The ablest and most prudent men among them
wished to prolong the ostracism, at least until the

Republic should have assumed something like a definite form and tolerable consistency. The unreasoning peasants of four departments shipwrecked the judgment and sagacity of these politicians. They elected Louis Napoleon to serve as their representative in the Legislative Assembly, and thus deprived the Provisional Government of the means of saving the country. Let no mystical partisans of Louis Napoleon affect to regard this as a proof of his superior abilities. His election recals strongly to my mind two lines of Pope describing the appearance of a popular actor on the stage :

> "Booth enters ; hark, the universal peal !
> But has he spoken ?　Not a syllable."

It is no joke, but a sober truth, which ought to make us blush for modern civilisation, that in some departments of France, the rustic inhabitants believed that Napoleon himself had once more returned. He had come back from Elba, why not from St. Helena or the Shores of Acheron ? They knew of no philosophy which forbade this supposition, Napoleon Bonaparte, Lucien Bonaparte, Pierre Bonaparte, and Louis Bonaparte, were all the same to them. They had never been taught to distinguish one from the other, the great from the little, the

little from the great, or even the living from the
dead.

They wanted a Bonaparte, man or mummy did
not much signify. The old sorceresses of the Pagan
world pretended that words had power to trans-
form the shapes of living creatures, to prolong or
shorten human existence, and even to bring down
the moon from her sphere. The rustic population
of France possessed a credulity equally potent.
The words Austerlitz, Jena, Eylau, Marengo, were
in their opinion sufficient to ensure the happiness of
thirty-six millions of people. They wanted a Republic, they had fought for a Republic, they had shed
their blood for a Republic ; but they wanted at the
same time a man between whom and the Republic
there existed the most irreconcilable enmity.

They elected him, therefore, as I have said, to
serve as one of their representatives in that legislative
Babel, the National Assembly. From that moment
the fate of the Republic was sealed. The skeleton
of Napoleon, already brought home from St. Helena,
rose from its grave to crush the fragile form of
liberty to death. The old man stood in the young
man, whom he had invested with artificial interest,
and enabled him to stifle the voice of freedom. The
fathers of the new Republic had proved themselves

T

to be weak and vacillating; weak in their conceptions
of government, vacillating in their determination
to defend what they had created. In order to
escape the charge of imitation, they would have
no senators, no upper house, which they imagined
would have brought their Republic into a too close
conformity with the constitutions of Great Britain
and America. They resolved to have something
new, and something new they had, — a monster with
nine hundred heads, and innumerable fangs with
which to tear to pieces the infant constitution.

This course they pursued in order to be purely
democratic. But by converting their legislature
into a mob, they rendered it incapable of united
and simultaneous action, and prepared for Louis
Napoleon, with other bold adventurers, abundant
means for subjugating the country. I heard at the
time the whole subject discussed by several members of the Provisional Government, who regarded
with ill-disguised contempt the tame liberty of
England, which they fully believed they should soon
eclipse and throw for ever into the shade.

Louis Napoleon encouraged the growth and
diffusion of this absurd belief. The new Republic
required a president. He was put forward as a
candidate for the presidentship. By all his friends

and partisans he was spoken of as the Prince.
Persons who called themselves Republicans imagined
they received some lustre from being associated with
the cause of a man upon whom such a title had
been conferred. On the one hand, nothing was
sufficiently democratic to satisfy the pretended republicanism of these Frenchmen, while, on the other,
nothing was sufficiently imperial to satisfy their
superstitious idolatry for rank and titles.

General Cavaignac, a real Republican from his
heart, a man of pure life and irreproachable honour,
was put forward by the best men in France as
candidate for the presidentship. If there had been
no emperors or princes in his family, there had been a
long line of great Republicans, true to their principles,
unconquerable in their fidelity. But even from
ancestors such as these he sought to derive no
claim to the suffrages of the French people. He
stood upon his own actions, upon his love of discipline, upon his protracted services, upon the glory
of many campaigns amid the burning wastes of Africa.
Recalled to serve his country at home, upon the
first establishment of the Republic, he had performed
his duty in very trying situations with the most un-
flinching valour and unbroken integrity. He therefore came forward in his own name, armed with his

own virtues, bright in his own honour, to ask permission of his countrymen to secure to them the inestimable blessing of free institutions.

If there be a man in Europe who resembles Washington it is General Cavaignac; and I have sufficient faith in human nature to believe that, had he been chosen to be the first President of the Republic, all would have gone well with France. This man however, so honourable, so true, so virtuous, so estimable in every sense of the word, still lives, and lives in France, over the whole of which his great merit sheds a lustre.

There was another candidate for the presidentship, who by a very considerable party was thought worthy to be preferred before Louis Napoleon—I mean Ledru-Rollin. In the stormy days of February, and all the turbulent agitations that succeeded, he had given proof of enlarged conceptions, of a liberal and daring policy, eloquence unequalled by any contemporary speaker, and indomitable firmness and courage. He appeared to revive in the nineteenth century the abilities and the enthusiasm of the old Revolution, and, had his honest counsels been followed, would have saved the Republic in spite of itself. He appeared to be actuated by a warm and generous philanthropy; he cared for the poor; he watched with earnest solicitude over the fortunes of the artisan and the labourer.

That he may have been ambitious also, I confess — for what statesman is not? But his ambition would have led him to serve France, to give her free institutions, and to wield the vast power she possesses for the benefit of all the depressed and suffering populations of Europe.

In the course of his political career, Ledru-Rollin has committed errors which may perhaps explain, if they do not justify, his present position. But the defects of his personal policy are clearly traceable to circumstances. Louis Napoleon committed much greater, but survived the effects of them, not so much through superiority of character as through the force of the Napoleonic element on which he floated into power. With equal good fortune, Ledru-Rollin would have exhibited greater mental resources. He is an exile, because he relied exclusively on his own qualifications for success, and these, though very remarkable, were not sufficient in the estimation of his countrymen to weigh down the merits of an opponent from the Bonaparte family.

When the names of the different candidates went forth into the country the whole French nation was shaken by contending feelings and opinions, though it soon appeared that an immense majority were determined to give their suffrages for Louis Napoleon. Several Republican writers, suffering their views to be influenced by their predilections, have endeavoured to explain away the phenomenon by an organised system of corruption, extensive enough to embrace the whole Republic. But no explanation of this kind will suffice to account for the fact. The truth, however unpalatable we may find it, appears to be, that a vast majority of the French people are strongly attached to monarchy, even when it assumes the form of despotism. When therefore they voted for Louis Napoleon, it was not with an eye to his continuing President of the Republic, but to his restoring the Empire. They derived their political inspiration from his uncle's acts and government; they were filled with reminiscences of military glory; they recalled the times in which French armies carried terror and desolation into nearly all parts of Europe; and they gave their votes to the nephew, in the hope of seeing those days renewed.

If these events had not passed before our eyes, we should hardly be able to believe in the existence of so much levity as was displayed in 1848 by a majority of the French people. They obviously did not reflect, while giving their votes, on the significance or importance of what they did.

By the proceedings of those days, the condition of France for many years to come was to be determined, and the progress of civilisation throughout the continent of Europe checked or advanced. Yet they suffered their passions to be thrown into a ferment by dazzling but futile reminiscences, forgot all the insults which had been offered to freedom by Napoleon, his general oppression of the poor, the injustice and tyranny of his imposts, the incurable disorder of the finances, the horrors of the conscription, the almost complete exhaustion of the resources of the country, the invasion of France by foreigners, the bombardment of Paris, the intense misery and desolation which, through his ambition and unprincipled policy, had been brought upon the whole country; — they forgot all these things, I say, and, through the influence of certain hallucinations about glory, voluntarily exposed themselves to the risk of being hurried again through the sufferings and disasters of a similar career.

CHAP. V.

LOUIS NAPOLEON PRESIDENT OF THE REPUBLIC.

By these facts we are forced into the melancholy inference that nations in the present state of the world are little suited to decide what is best for themselves. The greater number of men are often ready to sport with the prosperity of an empire, as if it were a toy or a plaything, and not the concentrated interests of many millions of families. France, however, has long been governed by the army. The people vote, but it is the army that gives a direction to popular feeling. Peasants, artisans, shopkeepers, may have their political opinions and be inclined to adhere to them; but half a million of men with swords in their hands, and ever ready at the bidding of their chief to sheathe them in the bodies of the people, must always give whatever direction they please to a popular movement.

The traditions of his family had secured to Louis Napoleon an unquestionable majority among the soldiers; and their suffrages determined those of the ploughmen, the vine-dressers, the masons, bricklayers, and carpenters, who constitute the mass of the rustic population in France. Well, Louis Napoleon was elected President of the Republic, and took an oath solemnly before God, and in the face of the French people, faithfully to administer and preserve the government, with the management of whose affairs he was entrusted. Victor Hugo, who was present, describes the ceremony in the following striking manner.

"It was about four in the afternoon. It was growing dark, and the immense hall of the Assembly having become involved in gloom, the chandeliers were lowered from the ceiling, and candles were placed upon the tribune. The President made a sign; a door on the right opened, and there was seen to enter the hall and rapidly ascend the tribune, a man still young, attired in black, having on his breast the badge of the Legion of Honour. All eyes were turned towards this man. His face wan and pallid, its long emaciated angles developed in prominent relief by the shaded lamps, — his nose large and long, — his upper lip covered with mustachios, — a lock of hair waving over a narrow forehead, — his eyes small and dull, — his attitude timid and anxious, bearing in no respect a resemblance to the Emperor; — this man was the citizen Charles Louis Napoleon Bonaparte.

"During the murmurs which arose upon his entrance he remained for some instants standing, his right hand in his buttoned coat, erect and motionless on the tribune, the front of which bore this date, 22nd, 23rd, 24th of February; and above was inscribed these words, Liberty, Equality, Fraternity.

"At length silence having been restored, the President of the Assembly struck the table before him several times with his wooden knife, and then, the last murmurs of the Assembly having subsided, said, 'I will now read the form of the oath. Thus it runs: "In presence of God, and before the French people, represented by the National Assembly, I swear to remain faithful to the democratic Republic, one and indivisible, and to fulfil all the duties imposed on me by the constitution."' The President of the Assembly, standing, read this majestic formula; then before the whole Assembly, breathlessly silent, intensely expectant, the citizen Charles Louis Napoleon Bonaparte raised his right hand, and said with a firm full voice, 'I swear.'

"The President of the Assembly, still standing, proceeded: 'We take God and man to witness the oath which has now been sworn. The National Assembly adopts that oath, orders it to be recorded with the votes, printed in the "Moniteur," and published in the same form and manner as the acts of the legislature.'

" The matter seemed now complete, and it was imagined that the citizen Charles Louis Napoleon Bonaparte, thenceforth until the second Sunday in May
1852 President of the Republic, would descend from
the tribune. But he did not ; he felt a magnanimous
need to bind himself still more closely if possible, to
add something to the oath which the Constitution had
demanded from him, in order to make a show how
largely this oath was in him free and spontaneous.
He asked permission to address the Assembly.
'Speak,' said the President of the Assembly ; ' you
are in possession of the tribune.' There was, if
possible, deeper silence and more intense attention
than before. The citizen Louis Napoleon Bonaparte
unfolded a paper, and read a speech. In this speech,
having announced and installed a minority, whom he
had already selected, he said :

" ' I desire in common with yourselves, citizen representatives, to consolidate society upon its true basis,
to establish democratic institutions, and earnestly to
devise the means calculated to relieve the sufferings
of the generous and intelligent people who have just
bestowed on me so signal a proof of their confidence.'

" But that which especially struck every mind,
which became profoundly graven in every memory,
which found its echo in every honest heart, was the

declaration, the wholly spontaneous declaration, let it
be borne in mind, with which he began his address :
' The suffrages of the nation, and the oath I have just
taken, command my future conduct. My duty is
clearly traced out ; I will fulfil it as a man of honour.
I shall regard as the enemies of the country all who
seek to change by illegal means that which entire
France has established.'

" When he had done speaking, the Constituent
Assembly rose and sent forth, as with a single voice,
the grand cry, ' Long live the Republic ! ' "

Here, then, had Louis Napoleon been possessed by
an honourable ambition, was the point to have arrived
at which should have satisfied him.   France was in
possession of a free constitution, imperfect no doubt,
but the imperfections it had   might   have   been
gradually removed.   He was now the first magistrate
of a great nation, and stood at the head of a government, the principles of which he had all his life professed to reverence.   No   position   could   be   more
proud.   The fame of Washington was within his
reach; the firm resolution to be   honest and to
fulfil the duties he had undertaken would have
linked his name for ever to the cause of freedom, and
have entitled him to the respect of all future times.

But the Bonaparte taint was in his blood, and the

Bonaparte immorality in his mind. To be within reach of a sceptre, and not to grasp at it, no matter by what means, was a pitch of virtue, the possibility of which he could not conceive. To set an example of political integrity would have appeared the height of weakness in his eyes. He converted Swift's joke into a reason of state, and, because posterity had done nothing for him, was determined to do nothing for posterity.

From the moment of his election, Louis Napoleon, it cannot be doubted, began to plot against the Republic, to tamper with the fidelity and corrupt the discipline of the army, to purchase partisans, and to take all practicable measures for building up his own fortunes upon the ruins of the state. It is not by any means my intention to write the history of France under Louis Napoleon's presidentship, but merely to trace his personal career, and to recapitulate the means by which he transformed the Republic into an Empire.

In the struggle against freedom which now succeeded, he was not strong with his own strength, but traded as usual with his uncle's name, and invoked the sinister shadows of St. Helena to aid him in subverting the constitution of his country. I am not unmindful of the old saying, that flattery begets

friends, while truth is repaid with hatred. Let it be
so. There must be somebody to speak the truth from
time to time, whatever may be the consequences to
him who utters it. The French are our neighbours,
our allies, and have been our companions in arms. It
will perhaps seem ungracious, therefore, to state
facts and make reflections which may appear to call
in question their honesty or good sense. But,
honouring them as I do for the sacrifices they have
made to deliver the human race from servitude, I
yet cannot be insensible to the fact that no nation in
Europe, taken as a nation, is so ready to be led
astray by names, by fictions, by the splendours
of wealth, or by the gorgeous blazonry of power.

The Dutch sacrificed their liberties to the puerile
vanity of having a prince for a stadtholder, and the
French, in like manner, have relinquished in our own
days all the advantages of a free government,
in order to be ruled by a prince of recent manufac-
ture, to have a court in Paris, and to behold the
revenues of the state lavished upon shows and the
architectural embellishments of the capital. They
have suffered their reason to succumb to the vulgar
delusion that a court enriches a country by its
profuse expenditure. If wealth came to the court in
showers from the firmament, and was then distri-

buted with a liberal hand among all comers, there might be some excuse for this vulgar error. But the court, in the first place, takes from the many what it afterwards disburses with unjust favouritism among the few. It creates nothing; it imports nothing by secret channels from foreign countries, except in the case of such rulers as Charles the Second, to whom bribes were given by neighbouring states. It only, according to the old adage, robs Peter to pay Paul.

But the French people are not sufficiently well versed in political economy to perceive the force of this reasoning. They look upon Louis Napoleon as a public benefactor because he has erected new streets in Paris, and thus, as they imagine, created employment for the workmen. In truth, however, he only causes that amount of capital to be expended on one point of France which, had he allowed things to pursue their natural course, would have been expended more profitably, perhaps, on other points.

But the perception of this truth appears to be beyond the range of French popular ideas. It is not the vocation of the multitude to reason; but, should it ever take this turn, immense changes will soon be effected in the world.

CHAP. VI.

HIS CONDUCT IN OFFICE.

ONE of the first acts of Louis Napoleon, after entering upon his office as President, was to demand of M. de Malleville, Minister of the Interior, the delivering up to him of all the documents relating to the affairs of Strasbourg and Boulogne. The minister refused, the President insisted, and the subject was brought before the Legislative Assembly, where de Malleville explained his reasons for ceasing to be a member of the government. This circumstance may be very differently regarded by different persons. Some look upon it as a result of the sense of shame, because they give the President credit for repenting sincerely his attempts against the crown of Louis-Philippe. It is more probable that a careful study of those papers would have brought to light facts irreconcilable with his new political profession of faith, and therefore he desired their destruction. He might have reflected, however, that a few inconsistencies, a few contradictions more or less, are not likely to make any difference in the estimate which posterity will form of his character and actions.

They who take the most favourable view of Louis Napoleon's proceedings at this time virtually admit that it was never his intention to keep the oath he swore to the Republic. They set up the consciousness of what they call his mission, against the pledge of political fidelity which he gave in presence of the Assembly. He had, we are told, numerous duties to fulfil: to restore confidence and self-respect to the army, humiliated by the events of February; to crush the spirit of liberty, under the name of Socialism; to destroy the independence of the legislature, and to preserve society from becoming liberal, enlightened, and free. It is wholly unnecessary in a work like the present to follow in chronological order the achievements of Louis Napoleon during his presidentship. They were all calculated to produce one result, and the sagacity which presided over them can scarcely be too much admired.

To accomplish his principal design, Louis Napoleon found it would be necessary to direct the energies of the people into a multitude of channels; to marshal on his side all influential and deep-rooted popular prejudices; to conciliate the Catholic party

U

by affording assistance to the Pope, whom he had formerly sought to dethrone; to win over the aristocracy by annihilating universal suffrage, and to cajole capitalists by making war upon those who, through the establishment of industrial associations, aimed at bettering the condition of the poor. He did not, of course, forget that he had himself once advocated in the most strenuous manner the organising of such associations. But that was when he was a prisoner in the citadel of Ham, and when he thought it would pave the way for the advancement of his ambition, to affect sympathy for the working classes. He now, through all possible channels, sought to diffuse a belief in the existence of a party aiming at nothing short of the entire destruction of society. The members of this party his organs were instructed to denominate Socialists, and to speak of them at all times as the enemies of property and order, of virtue and morality, of law, of government, of literature, art, science and civilisation; in one word, as cannibals, eager to massacre and devour their neighbours.

Here in England, many have believed that Louis Napoleon was unanimously elected by the French people, with a view to his becoming what he has since shown himself. Nearly all the facts

of recent French history point to a different conclusion. When, in the December of 1848, five
millions of votes were given for him, it was in
the hope that he would be the preserver, not the
destroyer of freedom. If his Socialist writings
had not been generally read, the fact that he
professed Socialist opinions was universally known.
The honest rustics, therefore, when they gave him
their suffrages, were very far from foreseeing
that they were setting up a master, who would keep
them down with a rod of iron, maintain all the
rigours of the passport system, multiply taxes, and
cause them to be paid at the point of the bayonet,
suppress all means of circulating ideas, put an end
gradually to the representative system, and, in the
language of his apologists, avenge the cause of
monarchy, and the death of Louis XVI.

The French people, in general, did not expect or
desire all these things; but then it must be added
that they did not know very exactly what they expected or desired. The word Republic sounded
well, and they persuaded themselves that it signified
a government subsisting altogether without taxation.
They saw no reason, moreover, why they should not
enjoy the empire at the same time. As many
of them as had read Louis Napoleon's writings were

aware that he always employs the words Republic
and Empire as synonymous terms. To avoid all
misapprehension, he states emphatically that his
principles are Republican, but that they can no
otherwise be developed than in the forms of
monarchy. This probably seemed clear to the Gallic
rustics, but for the benefit of politicians needs
a commentary. However, when men have sinister
objects in view, it would be impolitic to be perspi-
cuous. Ideas and opinions big with disaster to the
human race should be expressed, when they are expressed at all, ambiguously, darkly, in the style of
ancient oracles.

Louis Napoleon naturally took refuge in this mode
of writing in his " Rêveries," " Considérations,"
" Mélanges," and so on. People might follow his
words, but in order to pursue his real meaning, it
was necessary to possess keen powers of scent. The
trail went in no one direction over the grass, but
touched its summits here and there uncertainly at
intervals, by bounds and starts, as his wild logic
thought fit to steer its course to escape detection.
Accordingly the French, when they elected him as
President, took what may emphatically be called a
leap in the dark. They would and they would not.
Like all weak people, they liked a prince, but they

also liked a cheap prince, and the good honest folks
had learned to believe that Louis Napoleon possessed
Fortunatus's wishing-cap, and could obtain whatever
he desired, without laying imposts upon industry.

The great majority of mankind are never convinced by anything but experience. When Louis
Napoleon began his progresses, when he went from
city to city, from town to town, when he was careful
to be present at the opening of every new railway, at
civic banquets, at military reviews, at commercial
gatherings, where he always made speeches tending
to impress on the minds of his hearers the advantage
of military rule, and the maxims of a concentrated
despotism, the eyes of the nation were gradually
opened. Then slowly, and, I think, with reluctance,
the partisans of revolutionary principles began once
more to think of combining and agitating. The
Republicans, though overthrown, had not been annihilated. They looked back, they reckoned up their
sacrifices, they recapitulated the sufferings they had
undergone since the storming of the Bastile, and the
annihilation of the oubliettes of the gentle Louis
XVI., and determined to recommence for France
and for freedom a new series of struggles.

In the " Nemesis of Power " I have described the
machinery by which the leaders of the great Revo-

lution disseminated their doctrines, and sapped the foundations of tyranny. They had to deal with a comparatively rude system. The old Bourbon princes lived in the belief that heaven itself watched over their prerogatives, and that no man, however bold and daring, would venture to dream of the subversion of their throne. The events of 1793 undeceived them; but until then, their superstitious faith in their own divine right rendered it easy to conspire against them.

Louis Napoleon, whatever he might wish other persons to believe, had no such faith in his own pretensions; and, therefore, was much more on his guard. He saw that the political waters had been troubled, and that after many wild and tumultuous movements, the great currents of public opinion were setting strongly in against him. This time the operations of the propaganda were not carried on through books, or even through journals. The new secret societies kept no list of members, no record of their proceedings. They met, they spoke, they passed the word of liberty from mouth to mouth, and the passions and sentiments swelling in the great heart of liberty in Paris, originated a movement which went vibrating to the extremities of France, animating all ranks and conditions of men to combine against the new form of oppression.

It may be regarded as one of the most inexplicable facts in the history of modern society, that although the existence of this vast and complicated organisation is well known, the government has hitherto been totally unable to discover its chiefs, or to arrest its growth. For nearly seven years it has gone on spreading its branches through the country, and acquiring fresh strength every hour. Despotism, however, always begets these anomalous institutions. In the first place, the rulers in such forms of civil polity set the people the example of conspiring. Louis Napoleon's whole life, after his elevation to the Presidentship, was one continued plot, and in carrying it on, he had this advantage over his antagonists, that he could profusely employ the resources of the State in purchasing agents and partisans.

The Constituent Assembly had with great liberality fixed the salary of the President at twenty-four thousand pounds sterling a-year, nearly five times the sum paid to the President of the United States. For all legitimate purposes, such an annual income would have been sufficient. But the President immediately began to affect the style of royalty; created the nucleus of a court; filled the palace of the Elysée with men of broken fortunes, ready to risk everything in the hope of acquiring a commanding position in the world.

To supply the necessities of these individuals was not easy, and Louis Napoleon's resources soon came to an end. He applied, therefore, to the Assembly, and the Assembly, with highly criminal complaisance, doubled his salary, that is, raised it to forty-eight thousand pounds a year. Even this sum was small, compared with the necessities of the President. He had a scheme in view, which would require the co-operation of numbers, including men of remarkable capacity, with little virtue, but a prodigious appetite for gold. Again, therefore, Louis Napoleon found himself obliged to appeal to the generosity of the Assembly for the sum of one million four hundred thousand francs, and with suicidal facility the infatuated representatives of the people put this second powerful weapon into the hands of their enemy.

Encouraged by success, and persuading himself, not without reason, that no limits could be discovered to the weakness of the Assembly, he soon made a third application for very little less than two millions of francs. Too late the legislature became alarmed, and refused his demand; but his partisans, having by this time grown bold and shameless, set on foot a subscription to enable the President to annihilate every vestige of liberty in France. It sometimes happens, however, that ridicule accomplishes what reason attempts in vain. The wits of Paris went to work; they joked, they sneered, they laughed, they circulated satirical songs in manuscript, and the begging conspirator was constrained to suppress the subscription.

Meanwhile other preparations were made for accomplishing the great design. By the famous law of the 31st of May, introduced by the renegade Orleanist, Léon Fauchet, universal suffrage was suppressed. A new Assembly was then elected, and upon examination of its elements was found to contain a dangerous proportion of Bourbonists and Orleanists. Wisdom, divine and human, has pointed out to us the danger of a house divided against itself. The different sections of the legislative Assembly, proud of the majority which by uniting together they could always bring to bear against the government, now adopted that wretched policy which blind party zeal is almost sure to recommend. Intrigues were set on foot by one section for the Comte de Chambord, by another for the Comte de Paris, by a third for Louis Napoleon, while France and the Republic were almost without supporters. Against such an

Assembly, the President felt it would not be very difficult to carry on a war.

For awhile he was checked by one consideration: General Changarnier, an Orleanist, held the post of commander-in-chief, and as he had fought and gained many victories in Africa, it was apprehended that in a crisis he might sway the decisions of the army. Louis Napoleon resolved, therefore, either to win him over, or to dismiss him from his command. Having failed in the former design, he had recourse to the latter; and General Changarnier stood in the National Assembly a mere citizen, representing some small fraction of the French people.

At the same time innumerable arts were put in practice to overshadow the public mind with fears and prognostics of a reign of terror. Assassination became the common topic of the day. An immense conspiracy was said to have been organised at the Elysée, and men wearing poignards were thought to mingle in every society from the palace of the Assembly to the meanest café. Experience has shown that nothing reduces the mind to so pitiable a state of weakness as perpetual fear. By degrees the Parisians were scarcely able to sleep quietly in their beds. Daggers introduced themselves into their dreams; they suspected everybody. Mutual confidence was at an end : even the friends of liberty scarcely dared to meet together, through apprehension of treachery.

It must not, however, be supposed that these apprehensions of conspiracy rested on mere surmises. The rulers of France had something more solid to go upon. It was well known in Paris that the exiled families were actively at work beyond the frontiers, while their partisans in the Assembly performed their bidding at home. These men, the Republicans of the Morrow, as they were then designated, had in some cases been publicly invited to concur in drawing up the constitution, and through treachery had purposely introduced into it the principles of dissolution. They never meant it should last, and as far as in them lay rendered it impossible. There is no act of baseness to which such men will not descend, and pride themselves all the while upon their own perfidy, as if it were a display of patriotism.

They hated Louis Napoleon much, but they hated the Republic still more. The permanent establishment of the latter must quench the hopes of their chiefs for ever; whereas the elevation and rule of Louis Napoleon would still be favourable to the general cause of monarchy. He was a prince, if not their prince. Nevertheless, as soon as by their assistance, he had ruined the cause of freedom, they considered his mission accomplished, and thought it would be easy to deliver themselves from him. Both Bourbonist and Orleanist pretenders cherished therefore the most brilliant hopes, and all possible efforts were made to disseminate the belief that this Bonapartist usurper, as he was denominated, would be put down, to make way for a prince of the old moth-eaten Bourbon stock.

These were the plotters with whom for the moment Louis Napoleon had to contend, and they were every wit as little scrupulous as himself. Had their designs succeeded, he would probably have found himself in the dungeons of Vincennes, and the experience of Ham would have taught them the impolicy of keeping a pretender in prison. A sudden fit of apoplexy might have come to the aid of the sacred cause, and Louis Napoleon would have passed out of the world with much less *éclat* than the Duc d'Enghien. The Republicans, as I have said, conspired also, but in a different way. They satisfied themselves with appealing to reason and common sense; but as these are seldom a match for cavalry and artillery there was for the moment little to be apprehended from their machinations.

There were some houses in Paris, where a few
young men of extremely advanced opinions, met together to discuss the prospects of Socialism : I should
perhaps offend them were I to say that they derived
their political principles from our virtuous country-
man, Sir Thomas More.   There was nothing practicable, as there was nothing dangerous, in their views.
They desired fervently to render mankind happy, but
were not at all agreed respecting the means.   That
they hated Louis Napoleon could not be doubted, because he had destroyed the Republic, under pretence
of serving it.   For this they may have been ex-
cusable; but when they indulged the hope of
overthrowing his government by appealing to the
reasoning faculties of the Parisians, they committed
an extraordinary mistake.   The Parisians are impassioned, bold, enterprising, patriotic, but they are
not rational; accordingly all that Louis Napoleon
had to fear for the moment—I do not now refer
to the future — was from the dynastic oppositions.
This he himself thoroughly understood : it was
against them, therefore, that he began to think seriously of bringing all the force at his disposal to bear.

   While things were verging towards this point
Louis Napoleon, having carefully studied the men
about him, had drawn together and admitted into

his confidence four or five individuals, distinguished
for their abilities, and equally hostile with himself
to republican institutions: De Morny, Magnan,
Persigny, St. Arnaud.* With these alone he consulted, and made preparations for the *coup d'état*
which was long contemplated before it fell upon
the country. History, when it comes to review
calmly the events of those times, will acknowledge
the weakness of the Assembly, which had little
hold upon the country, either through the character
of its members, or the wisdom and salutariness of
its decrees.

---

* On St. Arnaud's return from Malromé to Paris, he met
on the platform of the railway station at Poictiers the well-
known statesman and historian Thiers, and they proceeded in
the same carriage, chatting about every subject but politics.
These two men were not often brought together, but when
they did meet, it was on remarkable occasions. They first saw
each other in the Place du Carousel on the 24th of February,
1848. Again, on the 17th of November, 1851, during the
debate on the subject of the questors, they supported opposite
interests in the Assembly. They were not, I believe, brought
into personal contact on the night of December the 1st, but
it was by St. Arnaud's order that Thiers was arrested, dragged
from his bed, and thrown into prison. During their little col-
loquy in the Poictiers railway carriage, neither of them could
look ahead three months, and foresee in what relation they
would then stand to each other. After this, they never met
again, though perhaps M. Thiers may have been present at
St. Arnaud's funeral.

With us, Parliament may almost be said to be the nation in miniature. Its roots spread far and wide to the remotest shores of our islands, through nearly every rank of society, and deriving nourishment and strength from all, send them up into the legislature, which thus becomes a power irresistible in its might, so that it never quails, or needs to quail, before any authority on earth. It was otherwise in France : they who were called the people's representatives in no sense represented the nation, which had, therefore, neither respect nor love for them. They besides made themselves the accomplices of the President in his attack on Rome, in his corruption of the army, in his ca-· pricious tampering with the suffrage, in his reckless and profuse expenditure of the public revenue.

When it came, therefore, to need the people's sympathy, the people sullenly withheld it. The trial of strength between the parliament and the President was made in the debate upon the demand of the questors to have an adequate guard assigned to the Assembly, to protect it against the chief of the state. Had success attended this attempt, a series of new complications might have been created, but the final result would have been the same, for the army and its officers had been bought over, and were ready to cooperate with Louis Napoleon in striking a fatal blow at public liberty.

It is generally admitted that there are some questions connected with this subject with which contemporary history must refuse to deal. In fact, the boldest pens shrink instinctively from the task. Let them remain therefore in the obscurity to which their moral character condemns them. Doubtless, however, there are persons at work, who through memoirs, diaries, letters written with closely locked doors at midnight, and involved in the mystery of cypher, will reveal to posterity what must remain hidden from us. Let us, however, proceed. We know enough to enable us to judge correctly of the character of Louis Napoleon, as well as to appreciate the merits and value of his instruments.

CHAP. VII.

THE COUP D'ÉTAT.

I HAVE said that a vast system of machinery had been for some time in operation, for the purpose of diffusing terror through society. Clarendon, when drawing a picture of our own civil war, suggests by one single anecdote a terrible idea of the state of things in London. " 1 went down," he says, " to the Parliament House, and met Oliver St. John at the door. I was perplexed and alarmed at beholding a smile on that grim and dark countenance, usually so calm and inscrutable. Something sinister to royalty I saw had happened. When I inquired how matters were proceeding, he replied in these ominous words: ' We must be worse, before we can be better.' "

All parties in France might now have adopted this phrase for their motto. It was evident that a crisis was approaching, and the only question was, whether liberty or despotism would be the result. Even this, however, was scarcely doubtful to those who could weigh Louis Napoleon and the Assembly

X

in the balance; the latter all weakness, vacillation, incertitude; the former all courage, resolution, and readiness for any crime.

To enter into details would be to write the history of France. I confine myself to what is personal. Having admitted into his confidence the four men of whom I have already spoken, he took measures with them for paralysing the strength of Paris, and rendering effectual resistance impossible. Great exploits, whether criminal or virtuous, require great resources for their development. Liberty alone rests upon the hearts and affections of men; despotism must everywhere be based on gold. The poor man who desires to trample on the laws of society is immediately crushed in the attempt. To succeed in this bold enterprise, it is necessary to approach the task enveloped in the impenetrable armour of opulence. Thoroughly comprehending this truth, Louis Napoleon conceived the grand idea of invading the Bank of France, and making himself master of its treasures. He had an illustrious example for an act of this kind. Julius Cæsar, when meditating the ruin of his country's liberties, broke into the Temple of Saturn, the bank of Republican Rome; and having possessed himself of the gold he found there, went on triumphantly in the career of despotism till the daggers of Marcus Brutus and his friends cut him short.

There is a mysterious power in money. Once in the possession of a million sterling, Louis Napoleon felt that he had all France at his feet. Nevertheless, it was necessary to employ this mighty instrument with policy ; and, by means of which we are as yet ignorant, he contrived to dazzle and subdue the soldiers with gold, just at the very moment when he required them to become his accomplices. To what extent the same subtle influence had been at work among the leading statesmen of France is not known. The Assembly became conscious that a gulf was opening under its feet, and sent a number of its members to confer at the Elysée with its arch enemy. The scene was pre-eminently curious and original. Probably the members of the deputation were actuated by two very distinct motives: first, a desire to penetrate the designs of Louis Napoleon ; second, by menaces slightly disguised, to deter him from attempting their fulfilment. They succeeded in neither of their objects. He had from a child been silent, reserved, impenetrable. Experience had taught him the value of the qualities bestowed on him by nature, which were never more serviceable to him than on the present occasion.

The deputation went away from the palace disappointed, irritated, confounded,— not, as some have supposed, to organise plots against the President,— which they knew too well could have led to nothing, — but to feel all the bitterness of a too late repentance. By subserviency and meanness of spirit, they had made him what he was, and now nothing was left them but to expiate, they knew not as yet how, the folly they had committed.

On the first of December, 1851, Louis Napoleon received at the Elysée the officers of all the regiments then in Paris. These men, quick to understand the exigences of power, perceived, from the style of their reception, that some display of energy was expected from them. The President had in his manner all the winning gentleness, all the fascination, all the graciousness of royalty. They beheld promotion in every smile, together with the badge of the Legion of Honour, and a glorious retirement for their old age. Their pulses beat quicker, their ideas of right and wrong became confused, and they resolved to look upon the President's enemies as their own. By a sort of military instinct not susceptible of explanation, they felt they were soon to be let loose against the people of Paris, and instead of recoiling from the idea, they hugged it passionately to their breasts.

The conspiracy now in progress was in every sense a military conspiracy. All that was practicable had been done to corrupt and win over the officers of the army. The few experienced and honourable men who had proved beyond the reach of bribes were superseded by younger generals, fetched expressly from Africa, and promoted over the heads of their superiors. Several of the chief conspirators were persons who lived in continual dread of their creditors, who had long lost character and caste, and were regarded by those who knew them as reprobates, inimical to society, because they had forfeited all title to its respect. But in enterprises like that in which Louis Napoleon was now engaged, men must make use of such instruments as are at hand. Speculators, intriguers, libertines, gamblers, were therefore welcomed at the Elysée, provided they displayed sufficient zeal and eagerness to unite in effecting the overthrow of free institutions. Money was the great lever by which these men of desperate fortunes were moved hither and thither by the President.

Experience, especially the experience of his own family, had taught him that most men in France

might be purchased, provided a sufficient sum were
offered them.   He himself has related, in illustration
of this truth, a curious and remarkable anecdote.

While the Congress of Vienna was sitting, Joseph, ex-king of Spain, having the most unbounded
faith in the venality of his countrymen, counselled
his brother Napoleon to insure the support of
Russia, by purchasing Count Pozzo di Borgo.   In
conformity with this advice, a friend, carrying five
millions of francs in his carriage, was despatched
post haste to the Austrian capital.   He arrived
towards evening, and without a moment's delay
called upon the diplomatist.   He was introduced:
he explained his business; but Pozzo di Borgo, in
mingled accents of regret and despair, exclaimed, " It
is too late!   I have spent the whole of this day in
prevailing on the Congress to outlaw Napoleon, and
place him for ever beyond the pale of diplomacy."

The imperial negotiator, however, having touched
adroitly on the five millions, gave a new direction to
the current of the Count's ideas.   He determined to
take the matter into consideration.   He went over
the ground a thousand times during that evening
and the succeeding night; but, in spite of his
ingenuity, stimulated and rendered fertile by the
thirst of gold, he could discover no pretext for

unsaying all that he had said in the Congress ; and
therefore, on the following day, was compelled to
acknowledge his inability to espouse the cause of the
fallen despot. " Had you arrived a few hours earlier,"
he said, " I might have saved Napoleon!"

Those five millions, then, had they been sent in
time, might have warded off the agonies of Malmaison,
the humiliations of Rochefort, and the dreary captivity of St. Helena. With a thorough knowledge
of these and similar facts, Louis Napoleon was
perfectly justified in speculating upon the purchase
of the army, which he undertook and accomplished,
with infinitely less difficulty, perhaps, than he expected to encounter.

To throw the Parisians off their guard, the
generals of the Elysée had for some time put in
practice a clever manœuvre. Several hours before
day, now earlier and now later, the troops marched
out with beat of drums from their barracks, and
proceeded in large bodies to the Champ de Mars,
ostensibly for the purpose of exercise. At first
these movements excited alarm, and the citizens
rushed half dressed to their doors and windows, persuaded the hour of the *coup-d'état* was come ; but
when, night after night, the same drum-beating and
tramp of horses were heard, without being succeeded

by any catastrophe, people became accustomed to the thing, and relapsed into their usual indifference. The Government so far had accomplished its purpose; and it now only remained to select the best moment for striking the blow.

Most of the necessary arrangements having been thus made, Louis Napoleon invited his four principal ministers to repair at a late hour to the Elysée. There the fate of France, for some years, was decided upon. The National Assembly was to be annihilated, the press was to be gagged, and the people of Paris were to be terrified into submission by an overwhelming military force. The conspirators sat up all night, and at four o'clock in the morning, St. Arnaud, Minister of War, wrote to his mother: " In two hours' time we shall be in the midst of a revolution, which I hope will save the country," — the phrase always employed by the Bonapartists, when they desire to express the ruin of liberty. " The insane, blind, factious Assembly will be dissolved. Paris will awaken in the morning, and the revolution will be accomplished! Some hundred arrests or so, the door of the Assembly shut, and all's done. I am waiting for the commander of the troops to give him my last orders. Everything is ready : the Ministry is changed, and I form part of the new one. The whole course of action, and the regulation of the material force depend on me."

The two hours ran on, and the cold grey dismal morning had not yet broken, when on a hundred walls and corners of streets revolutionary proclamations were seen posted up. They whose occupations compelled them to rise early, approached the mysterious placards, and, by the light of the half dying lamps, read as follows: —

" In the name of the French people, the President of the Republic decrees : —

" Art. I. The National Assembly is dissolved.

" Art. II. Universal suffrage is restored.

" Art. III. The French people are to assemble in their Comitia from the 14th of December to the 21st of the same month.

" Art. IV. Martial law is proclaimed within the limits of the first military division.

" Art. V. The Council of State is dissolved.

" Art. VI. The Minister of the Interior is charged with the execution of the present decree."

In another proclamation he sought to defend at length his offence against liberty, by indulging in a fierce attack upon the constitution, which undoubtedly contained many defects. But of these he was thoroughly aware when he put himself forward as candidate for the Presidentship, and when after his election he swore a solemn oath in presence of the National Assembly, and added to that oath a voluntary declaration to observe as sacred and inviolable the Republican form of government.

It by no means diminishes the guilt of Louis Napoleon, to contend that the constitution was so full of absurdities and contradictions, that it was quite impossible it should last, and that in fact its original framers — Bourbonists, Orleanists, Bonapartists, and Republicans — never meant that it should last. A real friend of his country would have laboured to introduce reforms. He had the example of England before him. Our constitution, in whatever it may be thought to have consisted, was at first imperfect enough; but growing with the nation's growth, and strengthening with its strength, it has been converted by degrees into one of the noblest monuments of human wisdom of which history makes mention.

There is no reason why the French people should not have built on the Constitution of 1848 a fabric of rational liberty. Few institutions are so bad as to be altogether incapable of improvement. Had Louis Napoleon been a patriot, he would have discovered the means of accomplishing, without violence and bloodshed, what was needed by the country, and have taken care not to lay himself open to the charge of doing what he did for his own aggrandisement, not for the freedom and prosperity of France. Instead of this, he subverted the government of which he was himself the chief, by means which it is impossible too severely to condemn. He had then the hardihood, in a public document, to speak of the Constitution fiercely and vindictively as a dangerous enemy. When he asked the French people to make him President by their votes, it was obviously that he might stand at the head of the Republic; but when he had overthrown that Republic, and entrapped and imprisoned its defenders, he was not ashamed to adduce the very fact of his election as a proof that the country was adverse to the Constitution.

Six millions of votes, he says, were a strong protest against it. Yet when the nation was required to vote, the form of government was not in question — that had been previously settled, — and the business then in hand was simply to choose a man who, in conjunction with others, might manage public affairs. This, it appears to me, is a fair and impartial statement of the case. I am incapable of viewing it in any other light; and by indulging in sophistry, sarcasm, invective, and misrepresentation, Louis

Napoleon proves that it surpassed his ingenuity to defend by any other means what he had done.

To proceed, however, with the narrative. Louis Napoleon had by decree dissolved the National Assembly ; but that body, becoming bold too late, resolved not to die quietly ; yet every step it now took, while it proved its innocence of conspiracy, proved at the same time its incapacity and want of foresight. French public men must always be regarded more or less as tragic or comic actors. They look upon themselves as on the stage, and are persuaded that they have the whole world for their audience. This inspires them with the energy to perform occasionally brilliant actions, but oftener betrays them into bustle, rhodomontade, and intolerable exhibitions of arrogance.

What the National Assembly was to do, in the emergency which had suddenly arisen, nobody could decide ; but it determined, at all events, to meet and talk, which would be some consolation. Large bodies of members therefore hurried towards the Legislative Palace, but there discovered, to their dismay, that the President had been beforehand with them. Instead of admiring crowds, eager to listen to their eloquence, and disposed to respect in them the majesty of the French people, they encountered

regiments of drunken soldiers, who, without the
slightest regard to their senatorial character, hustled
and pushed them about in the most insolent manner.

Not being able to enter the edifice in the ordinary
way, they sought to steal in by the side-doors, but
were everywhere met by portions of the military
rabble with fixed bayonets. Jeered, scoffed, laughed
at, and humiliated, these manufacturers of decrees and
worshippers of ancient dynasties rushed angrily away
to the Mairie of the Tenth Arrondissement where
they resolved in their wrath to perform great things.
Rage prevented them from perceiving that they were
caught like so many mice in a trap ; that their efforts
would be of no avail, since the moment for action was
over, and that Louis Napoleon now regarded their
resentment with as little anxiety as that of any other
portion of the rabble. In preferring the interest of
princes before that of their country they had forfeited
all title to the nation's reverence, and condemned
themselves to witness the triumph of a dashing
usurper, who despised them for that very faithlessness
towards the Republic which had enabled him to
accomplish its ruin.

Having assembled, however, in the Mairie, to the
number of about three hundred, they proceeded in a
noisy and confused manner to vote the deposition of

Louis Napoleon. The speakers were numerous, in-temperate, fierce, clamorous; but among them all, one man only really experienced solicitude for the fate of the Republic; the others had their idols beyond the French frontier — Bourbons of the elder or younger branch, Counts of Chambord or Counts of Paris, Joinvilles, Aumales, Nemours, empty names and powerless frivolities compared with the iron phalanxes of the usurper in possession. Berryer, who had de-fended his offence at Boulogne, because it was only perpetrated against the younger branch, but which Louis Napoleon himself afterwards condemned as treason against the State,— Berryer, I say, now de-luded himself into the belief that his sonorous com-monplaces could rouse the people of Paris into the defence of a fragment of the Assembly.

Accordingly, in company with another person, he emerged through a window, and standing on a narrow balcony, addressed the multitude below, composed almost entirely of Republicans. No one there felt any sympathy for M. Berryer, who had been the ad-vocate of the Bourbons for half a century : yet when he spoke, the crowd listened ; until, turning round to a little bustling, fussy, mean-looking individual by his side, he exclaimed, " This is the man upon whom the National Assembly has conferred the command of the army,—it is General Oudinot ! "

At that name, so hostile to liberty and indissolubly associated with the fratricidal attack on the young Republic of Rome, the people burst in shouts of bitter and derisive laughter, which might speedily have proved the prelude to much more vigorous demonstrations of dislike, but that at the moment a number of strong arms were thrust out through the window, and in an instant the orator and the General disappeared, and a row of bayonets flashed along the balcony. In fact, while this section of the Assembly was in the midst of its deliberations, a large body of infantry had broken into the edifice, with loaded muskets, fixed bayonets, and furiously drunk. Resistance was impossible, and these infatuated partisans — Bourbonists, Orleanists, Fusionists, who, by their culpable intrigues, had brought about the ruin of the Republic — were marched off, under a strong escort, and with few or no tokens of sympathy from the people, to the prison of Mont Valerian and the château of Vincennes.

It was now generally felt that, for a time at least, the political game was up. Fifty thousand men — infantry, cavalry, artillery — were posted in different parts of Paris, ready at the slightest signal from the Elysée, to cut down or blow to atoms any who should dare to raise a cry for the Republic. The suddenness of the blow had paralysed the courage

of the Parisians. Everybody feared everybody.
Friends, relations, wives, children, brothers, were
suspected. According to public opinion, wherever
five men were assembled, one of them was sure to be
a spy. Men of decided Republican principles, who
were generally known, now suddenly disappeared;
bodies were found in the Seine, in deserted houses,
in unfrequented places, in the city, and in the suburbs.*

This was the commencement of a Reign of Terror,
and during many hours, fear the most abject pervaded the whole body of society. But the Republicans, though they entertained no hope of success,
were determined that free institutions, however imperfect, should not perish without being hallowed by
the blood of some at least of their defenders. They
therefore, with hopeless valour, descended into the
streets to die. The traditions of the eighteenth century were deeply engraven on their hearts, with all
that France had done and all she had suffered for
liberty.

They spread themselves through the city, they
carried about journals printed in secret, they col-

* For a vivid picture of the interior of the French capital,
during those days, see " Purple Tints of Paris," ii. 301—330.

lected crowds, they delivered harangues, fiery, but
full of the melancholy accents of death. The blood
of the Republican youth was once more kindled, and
the general cry was, " To the barricades ! " " to the
barricades ! " These words thrilled to the heart of
Paris, and during the night of the third, hundreds of
those dreadful fortifications of liberty sprang up in
the streets as if by magic. There is a limit, however,
to the efforts of human courage. The Republicans
were few, dispersed, taken by surprise, destitute of
leaders. But they could always die, and die they
did gallantly, behind the barricades, and with their
blood the flame of freedom was extinguished, if not
for ever, at least, for many years, in France.

CHAP. VIII.

THE MASSACRE OF DECEMBER.

THE 4th of December, big with disaster and calamity, dawned like a day of doom upon Paris. In the Fasti of the Roman Republic, the day on which the soldiers of the commonwealth fell at Allia was not more deserving to be linked with dismal associations. Masses of soldiers, infuriated with brandy, extended in long lines through the great thoroughfares, to intimidate or slaughter the population. Louis Napoleon felt that it was possible to break the spirit of France, by deluging the streets of Paris with blood, and extirpating as far as possible all the Republicans.

Suddenly, on the Boulevards, when the thronging and excited passengers least expected it, a pistol was fired, by whom is not known. The soldiers immediately presented arms, a line of flame passed along the streets followed by the report of musketry, and the shrieks of men, women and children rolling upon the earth in mortal agony. The soldiers again loaded their pieces, and raked the windows and balconies of the opposite houses, killing indiscriminately all who presented themselves. The streets were encumbered with the dead; the kennels ran red with blood; here the grey hairs of age were dabbled in the gory puddle, and there infants crawled over the dead bodies of their mothers. The drunken soldiers proceeded with their butchery until nothing that had life was seen in the streets. The corpses were then heaped together, and borne pell-mell to the cemetery of Montmartre, where they were buried with their heads above ground; ostensibly, that their relatives might recognise them, but really, in order to inspire the most bewildering fear into the minds of the Parisians. How long those ghastly grinning heads were suffered to remain in that situation is not stated, but they disappeared by degrees, though not until the people of Paris had learned thoroughly to comprehend the Napoleonic idea, and the sort of blessings it is calculated to bring along with it.

The victory over the people had been gained in Paris, but the provinces still remained to be subdued. Risings took place simultaneously in various departments, but the army, the ready instrument of oppression, was everywhere at hand to crush the scattered insurgents. No people on earth are so bitter against each other as the French when they differ on political or religious grounds. They then set no bounds to their ferocity: victors and vanquished heap upon each other for the present time, and transmit in memoires to posterity, the most fearful calumnies.

According to the Napoleonists, the provincial insurgents all over France were odious savages, who delighted in crime, and had no other object in taking up arms. But they who circulated such reports lent them no credence. They knew them to be mere fabrications, intended to serve the purposes of despotism, for being transmitted to foreign countries by the organs of government — and no others were suffered to exist — they would at least appear to justify the rigorous measures taken to repress popular commotions.

No exact record has perhaps been kept of the massacres by which Louis Napoleon celebrated his inauguration as President for ten years. They supplied the place of those rejoicings by which the change of governments is sometimes commemorated in other countries. But from that time to this no means has existed of getting at the truth, because the freedom of the press being totally destroyed, the whole French people grovel in mental darkness, scarcely beholding the grim idol, which, according to the organs of the Tuileries, they worship with the most profound devotion.

When Louis Napoleon abolished the freedom of the press, he stated his reason to the senators and deputies of his new constitution. Those reasons are always on the lips of despotism, that is to say, the abuses and inconveniences which must always accompany full liberty of speech. He recognised his incapacity to regulate journalism in France, and therefore destroyed it. Formerly, when writing on the affairs of Switzerland, he had made use of the following words: " Every citizen of a Republic must desire to be free, and liberty is a vain word unless it be practicable to express unrestrainedly in writing a man's thoughts and opinions. If the press experienced obstructions in one canton, it would betake itself with its enlightenments and blessings to another; and the canton which should have excluded it would not be at all the more secure against its attacks. The liberty of the press ought therefore to be general."

Reflection on this passage must surely inspire the French people with a mean idea of their own character. Their emperor himself has informed them, that in every country where the press is not free, liberty is a vain word. By his own logic, therefore, they are slaves, and must now derive what comfort they can from that circumstance.

From this time forward the history of Louis Napoleon, losing all individual interest, becomes the history of France, which it is not by any means my intention to write. Besides, since no free press exists under his government, it is impossible to collect materials which can be relied on. Yet the career of Louis Napoleon, though its characteristics be totally changed, still possesses a deep interest, and is fraught with instruction moral and political.

The Republic having been destroyed in December 1851, he immediately set about completing the task which he had proposed to himself, namely, the reconstruction of the Empire. This had been his object from the beginning, but his means varied according to his position. For awhile, even after the *coup d'état,* he sought to conceal his aim, though in this he was not successful, because most persons perceived distinctly what he meant to accomplish, though no one possessed the power to thwart his designs. In the situation in which he had now placed himself, it was obviously his policy to strike while the iron was hot; during the terror which succeeded the massacre he issued orders and decrees, which fell rapidly like

heavy blows upon the French people, and terrified
them into the most servile submission. To show
any active opposition to the government was death,
and to convince men that his menaces were not so
many vain words, the slightest pretext was seized
upon for having recourse to military executions. He
printed the phrase " Vive la République " at the top
of all his proclamations, but if any Frenchman, encouraged by his example, shouted the same words in
the street, he was seized and shot like a dog upon
the pavement.

Then appeared the denunciations against socialism
and secret societies, to have belonged to which at any
time rendered a man liable to transportation. By
this edict two millions of persons at least were placed
within the fatal grasp of the government, and might
at any moment be torn from their families and their
homes and sent to Algeria or Cayenne. The process was actually commenced on a grand scale.
Eight thousand Republicans were arrested, and
numbers of them having been allowed to pine and
perish in French dungeons, the remainder were
sent like the refuse of humanity to manure the soil
of the colonies.

In the midst of these fearful scenes Louis Napoleon
vigorously pushed on his election. Orders were sent

down to all the prefects and military commanders in the provinces to see that everything was done to secure a vast majority. The voters were forbidden to use the ballot. They were to give their suffrages openly, and the enthusiastic Bonapartists set the example of coming to the poll with their votes pinned upon their hats. The electors with the fear of Cayenne and Algeria in their minds, marched to the urns between double rows of fixed bayonets. And thus, sixteen days after the massacre, Louis Napoleon was rendered complete master of France.

Foreign nations had long arrived at the conviction that the French people are incapable of liberty, and must therefore be subjected to despotic authority. It was accordingly a matter of indifference to them whether a Bourbon, an Orleanist, or a Bonapartist were at the head of affairs, since they considered it quite clear that some one invested with absolute power must occupy that place. To most of the governments of the continent this conviction was rather satisfactory than otherwise, and even here in England people had grown so weary of the perpetual revolutions which took place in France that they almost ceased to attach any importance to the form of government which might be established there. But they were not altogether without uneasiness at the success of Louis Napoleon, because they could not rid themselves of the idea that he had inherited the animosity of his uncle towards this country.*

For a considerable time this persuasion gained ground, and it seems perfectly certain that the French army as a body was animated by a very strong desire to avenge the disaster of Waterloo. How far Louis Napoleon shared this sentiment will perhaps never be exactly known, because circumstances at length occurred which gave a different turn to his speculations, and even inspired the whole French people with the desire to form a strict alliance with England.

After the *coup d'état* and the massacre of December, Louis Napoleon, as I have said, was re-elected President of the Republic, and this time not for four, but for ten years. He had not in vain read

---

* If any opinion can be formed from the tenour of Louis Napoleon's writings and speeches, his hatred of England has always been exactly in proportion to the magnitude of the benefits he has received from it. When pleading for his life in 1840, before the Chamber of Peers, he said "Je représente devant vous un principe, une cause, une défaite. Le principe, c'est la souveraineté du peuple; la cause, celle de l'empire; la défaite, Waterloo." Wouters 320. Several years before, he had observed in his "Considérations sur la Suisse" (Œuvres, ii. 371), that if ever France should avenge the battle of Waterloo, the liberties of Europe would be strengthened.

the history of France. He knew that although a fortunate general, or a legitimate pretender, or a profound intriguer might raise himself to sovereign authority, public opinion immediately began to alienate itself from him, that discontents arose, that plots were formed, that new ambitions sprang to light, and that in this manner governments crumbled away, and were dissolved. He determined to do all in his power to avoid such a catastrophe. But the whole extent and nature of his exertions have not been brought to light. His friends and ministers dispersed themselves over the country, sometimes ostensibly in search of health, sometimes for the transaction of official business, but in truth always for the single purpose of preparing men's minds for the restoration of the Empire.*

The real partisans of the Republic were everywhere denounced as socialists, drunkards, rabble, cannibals. The imperial press swarmed with the most odious accusations against immense sections of the community. Yet when it came to sum up, it

---

* On the 29th March, 1852, he delivered to a body of his creatures, assembled under the name of senators and deputies, in the palace of the Tuileries, a long and artful speech, in which he enumerated his reasons for not restoring the Empire. If, however, those reasons were valid then, they altogether ceased to be so eight months later. (Œuvres, iii. 325.

invariably decided that all France longed for the Empire as the only pledge of external peace and internal tranquillity.

To make trial of the feelings of the country Louis Napoleon undertook a sort of tour of examination which by many journalists was dignified at the time with the name of a royal progress. The préfets, the mayors, the military commanders, and all the other authorities of the several provinces had long received their instructions. In ways properly understood only by those functionaries, they excited the enthusiasm of the people, bringing forward all those who expected any favours however slight, and repressing and driving into the background all in whom Republican principles were known to have survived the trials of the last four years.

France, as one of the panegyrists of Louis Napoleon observes, is fond of glory, especially when contemplated from afar. Already the public had begun to forget what tears and blood had been shed for those victories which were now become so many immortal memories cast in bronze and brass as the imprescriptible titles of France to the sovereignty of the world! But it is easier to imitate the language than to revive the virtues, the power, and the institutions of ancient Rome. France never has been, and never will be mistress of the world, and her claims to be so considered provoke nothing save ridicule beyond her own frontier. But by encouraging these vain opinions, the members of the Bonaparte family have always contrived to stand high in public favour.

Louis Napoleon now went forth to gather the fruits of more than half a century of victories, blandishments and intrigues. Everything practicable had been done to excite alarms, and panic terrors connected with the spirit of socialism, represented as a political monster with a thousand heads, panting to assail and drain the blood of civil society. Between the triumph of this terrible phantom and the re-establishment of the Empire lay the only choice of France. The priests and the religious orders, diffusing themselves noiselessly, like a dark cloud over the land, excited the superstition of the people, and inspired them with the belief that religion was in danger.

In various parts of his writings, Louis Napoleon, not foreseeing that he might some day stand in need of it, speaks with profound contempt of this sacerdotal agency. After the great troubles of France which closed the eighteenth century, the clergy, he observes, were divided in two bodies, one consisting

of those priests who supported the new government,
the other composed of such as were refractory.
These, "the cherished children of the Pope," whose
rule he elsewhere denominates "a brutal despotism,"
profiting by the support extended to them by the
chief of their religion, exerted all the influence they
possessed in misleading the populace by their writings, which they poured from foreign countries into
France. In another passage he says, " Unhappily
the ministers of religion in France are generally
opposed to the interests of the people ; and therefore
to suffer them without control to establish schools
would be to permit them to instil into the popular
mind the hatred of liberty and the Revolution."

Now, however, he stood in need of these enemies
of freedom, who, on their part, readily became his
emissaries in raising the hackneyed but terrible cry
of " the Church in danger."   But the priesthood is
often found to be a two-edged sword, which alternately wounds both people and princes.   Thus we
are told that Verger, the detestable assassin of the
archbishop, ventured, in his fierce enthusiasm, to
raise his indignation even to Louis Napoleon ; for
in his letter to him he says, " Take heed to yourself."
Fanatical priests have in all ages been dangerous
enemies, and Verger perhaps had been studying the
passages I have quoted.

CHAP. IX.

THE PROGRESS.—THE EMPIRE.

THERE is always hope for a country when it can be roused to exertion by the idea that any peril is impending over its faith. But it argues the possession of little useful knowledge by the French people, to have been so easily persuaded, as they were in 1852, that Christianity had really anything to fear from socialism. However, the instruments I have mentioned were now unscrupulously employed in the service of Louis Napoleon, who sought personally to obtain an earnest of the people's suffrages in all provinces of France lying between Paris and the Mediterranean.

Great efforts have been made to create and diffuse through Europe the belief that on this occasion nothing was anywhere discoverable but the most enthusiastic loyalty. St. Arnaud, who accompanied him, was at first deceived by appearances. The students of English history will call to mind the prodigious outbreaks of enthusiasm which greeted

the younger Charles Stuart on his return from exile.
Louis Napoleon's companions for awhile imagined
they were witnessing a similar spectacle. He himself
seems never to have been deluded for a moment.
He understood his countrymen, and knew what their
shouts were worth. However, at Bourges, at Nevers,
at Moulins, at Grenoble, nothing was heard but
" Vive Napoléon ! " " Vive l'Empereur ! "

But as they proceeded the sky darkened, and
there were persons in Louis Napoleon's suite who
observed that in those southern provinces enthusiasm
often came forward to mask the approach of fanaticism, the word by which they designated Republicanism. They felt they were moving through a
sultry atmosphere, and that the thunder was gathering, though no clouds as yet appeared. The Minister
of War was filled with apprehensions, and scarcely
believed in his own power to ward off danger from
the decennial President by all the military arrangements he could make. The conviction became
stronger and stronger, as they approached the sea,
that they were treading over the ashes of a volcano,
which at any moment might explode, and blow them,
as the Minister of War expresses it, into a better
world. He, no doubt at the moment, felt he had
done his best to make this as bad as possible. It was

evident that a vast conspiracy existed, having its centre no one knew where, and spreading its ramifications no one could divine how closely, or how far.

The Minister's panic went on perpetually increasing. The blood shed on the fourth of December lay heavy on his soul. His days were uneasy, his nights disturbed. Louis Napoleon himself took refuge in his constitutional apathy, which after all was only the apathy of a mask, concealing the muscular indications of terror, which nevertheless stung and tortured him within. At Marseilles, still filled with reminiscences of the old Republic, a grand demonstration organised by the authorities awaited the candidate for the imperial throne ; the people by tens of thousands crowded the streets, the quays, the squares; there were cries of " Vive l'Empereur ! " nosegays were showered in abundance on the courtiers. But the faces of the crowd wore a strange expression. They did not appear to be looking at anything before them, but at somebody or something which was to come. Suddenly, amid piles of roses, there was discovered an infernal machine, which, in a few minutes, perhaps in a few seconds, would have exploded, and blown all within reach to atoms.

This little incident disturbed the economy of the President's ideas, and his Minister of War keenly felt how immense was the responsibility of his situation. He made many pompous professions, he used many big words, he repeated the boast of Bossuet to Louis Quatorze, and said he would defend the President's life with his own body. Nevertheless the pleasure of the progress was spoiled. No one exactly knew to whom, or to what party, this tremendous invention was to be attributed. It might be the Orleanists, it might be the Legitimists, it might be the Socialists. At any rate the fact had now become manifest, that the people of the South were dangerous. With no little precipitation therefore was the rest of the triumph hurried over. Their progress became much more progressive, and with chastened feelings mingled with dark forebodings Louis Napoleon and his Minister of War returned to Paris.

Notwithstanding the occurrence of these untoward events, the restoration of the empire was determined on, and the remainder of the year devoted to conciliating the courts of Europe. Some writers, hostile to Louis Napoleon at all stages of his career, call in question his talents. But what purpose can this serve? If his talents be below

z.

mediocrity, what must we think of those who suffered themselves to be overreached and put down by him? To adopt a French idiom, I would say of two things one, — either Louis Napoleon's genius and statesmanship are above the middle term, or those of his antagonists are very much below it. For myself, I by no means question his remarkable abilities or his knowledge, which, to confess the truth frankly, is greater than that of any other person who at this moment sits on a throne in Europe.

Within the sphere of this knowledge I place his acquaintance with that art which enables men to read each other, to separate the original and highly gifted thinkers from those who depend chiefly on their acquisitions, or their rank, or the traditions of place, family, or employments. He had a great deal of peculiar work to do, and with admirable tact he chose the proper men to do it. He understood moreover, extremely well, the habit of mankind, when they are called upon to judge the actions of persons in power, and foresaw how lenient they would prove to the excesses of his ambition. In 1852, on the anniversary of the *coup d'état*, he caused himself to be proclaimed Emperor, and obliterated from the public acts of France the very name of the Republic.

The state of the country since that period, it is
impossible to describe. In a mitigated form, it has
been one continued reign of terror. Any man's
house may be entered at any moment, his most
secret cabinets may be searched, his papers — even
the letters of his wife and children, his marriage
settlement, or the title deeds to his estate — may be
seized, sealed up, and carried for examination to the
office of a commissary of police. Nothing is held
sacred. Louis Quatorze, it is well known, used to
get the letters of his subjects intercepted by the
police, scrutinised, assorted, and arranged for his
perusal. Louis Napoleon does the same, but
instead of reading them himself he delegates the
task to his creatures.

For some time after the proclamation of the Empire
it remained altogether uncertain what course the
French Government would pursue with respect to
this country. A great deal of talk existed about
the invasion of England, and it may be regarded as
certain, that a large portion of the French army
looked forward to the incidents of the expedition
with no little hope and enthusiasm. The pillage
of London was regarded as a thing quite within the
limits of probability. The idea, whether entertained

by the Government or not, arose out of the declaration of Louis Napoleon, that he had the defeat of Waterloo to avenge. In all likelihood he never seriously meditated entering upon so Quixotic an enterprise, yet he adroitly contrived to insinuate the belief into the minds both of the French and the English people.

On this side of the Channel the French invasion constituted for a considerable time the leading topic in all companies; and the Government, urged by Parliament, took precautions for protecting our shores.

By degrees, another subject arose to absorb the mind of Europe. Russia, ever since the general peace, had been cherishing immense plans of aggrandisement, developing its frontier on the east and south, menacing the integrity of Turkey, and meditating, it was supposed, formidable encroachments on the territories of Germany. All its resources had been applied to the creation of an army of unparalleled magnitude, and innumerable emissaries, salaried by the Court of St. Petersburg, insinuated themselves into every country in the west and south of Europe, where they laboured to create the belief that the power of Russia was irresistible.

By these means, the ideas and opinions of the masses were subjugated; and when that process has been completed, the material subjugation of states often follows as a matter of course. Between the Court of St. Petersburg and the British Government there took place, about this time, a curious correspondence. The object on the part of Russia was to obtain the connivance of the Western Powers, while she consummated her designs against the Ottoman Porte. England she sought to win over by bribes; Austria she reckoned upon keeping still by menaces; and ever since the elevation of Louis Napoleon, France in her eyes appeared little better than a political nonentity. That this was a grievous error it needs no subtle reasoning to show; but the Czar nevertheless fell into it, and spoke of Napoleon the Third as an individual hardly worth the trouble of being consulted. The refutation of this opinion was afterwards written with blood and fire on the ruins of Sebastopol; but legitimate sovereigns, until they are taught better by experience, are apt to look upon parvenus with more contempt and dislike than are reconcilable with sound judgment.

Turkey had long been accustomed to endure with calmness the insolent threats of Russia. She believed profoundly in her own weakness, and had not much faith in the politicians of Western Europe. The Russian ambassador at Constantinople, inflated with pride and arrogance, had brow-beaten and terrified the Divan, and there appeared to be little reason to doubt, that a campaign suddenly undertaken and conducted with vigour, would carry the double-headed eagle to the Golden Horn. A bold and skilful diplomacy had sown distrust and apprehension in all the great capitals of Europe; many continental statesmen lived in affluence upon roubles from St. Petersburg, and writers of no mean talents had conjured up vast phantoms of Russian armies and Russian power in the minds of the ignorant and timid throughout Christendom.

Even Louis Napoleon, an author as well as an emperor, had suffered himself to be carried away by the belief in Muscovite omnipotence, and in two remarkable passages with which the inmates of the Winter-palace were, doubtless, familiar, had assigned to the czars the glorious task of regenerating the East. Into this theory he was partly perhaps betrayed by that sleepless jealousy of England from which no Frenchman is free. But when he gave vent to the opinion he was a private man, writing, if not for his bread, at least in the hope of earning a reputation.

His ideas in the estimation of kings and czars had then but little significance, but when he came to occupy a different situation his notions also were regarded differently. The world, in general, and regal personages more especially, value the thought for the person, not the person for the thought. A sceptred expression has tenfold the force of much wiser words from the lips of an obscure philosopher.

However this may be, it is probable that on the eve of the Russian war, Louis Napoleon earnestly wished he had never maintained the hypothesis, first briefly thrown out in the Napoleonic Ideas and afterwards at greater length in his pamphlet on the Canal of Nicaragua. In the former work, after strongly eulogising the despotism of the czars, he observes, "that the East can receive from Russia alone the improvements of which it stands in need." This passage supplies a key to the following, which without it would be unintelligible. Having spoken of several renowned emporiums, he remarks: "There exists another city famous in history, though now fallen from its ancient splendour, whose admirable situation renders it an object of attention to all the great powers of Europe, which agree to uphold a government there, less fitted in their opinion than *another* to profit by those advantages which nature has lavished upon it. The geographical position of Constantinople rendered it the queen of the ancient world. Occupying the central point between Europe, Asia, and Africa, it might again become the commercial entrepôt of all three, and acquire over them an immense preponderance. Lying between two seas resembling two great lakes, of which it commands the entrance, it might keep up in them the most formidable fleets, safe from the attacks of the whole world, and through these armaments establish its sovereignty over the Mediterranean and the Euxine. Mistress also of the mouths of the Danube, which would facilitate her entrance into Germany, and of the sources of the Euphrates, which would lay open the approaches to India, she would be in a position to dictate laws to the commerce of Greece, France, Italy, Spain, and Egypt. This is what the proud city of Constantine might be; and this is what it is not, because, according to Montesquieu, the re-establishment of an empire which would threaten the equilibrium of Europe cannot enter into the minds of the Turks."

No political reader can fail to perceive the bearing of this passage; but when it actually came to be a question whether Constantinople should remain in the hands of the Osmanlis or pass into those of the regenerating Russians, Louis Napoleon threw the brilliant sword of France beside that of England into the scales to prevent the realisation of his youthful theory.

CHAP. X.

THE RUSSIAN WAR.

HAVING so far succeeded, the Czar Nicholas Ro-
manoff suddenly determined to cross the Pruth, and
invade the Turkish empire. This movement was in
direct opposition to the policy of England, which it
is well known has always regarded Turkey as one of
the oldest and firmest of its allies. The idea immediately arose, therefore, of an Anglo-French alliance,
and Louis Napoleon was easily persuaded to co-operate
with this country in preserving that balance of power
upon which the civilisation of Christendom reposes.
One of the chief arguments employed to convince
his imperial mind, is said to have been this: in
language highly diplomatic and courteous, he was
given to understand that England was bent upon the
war with Russia, and would unquestionably undertake it, for the defence of the Osmanli frontier, whether with or without allies. That it would be his interest to join with Great Britain was clearly implied
in this fact, that it would be easy for us, by the ex-

penditure of a little money, to raise in France the standard of the Comte de Chambord, or the Comte de Paris, and bring about a Bourbon or an Orleanist restoration. The argument may not have been categorically stated, but it was suggested to the mind of Louis Napoleon, who immediately understood all the advantages which would arise to him from the friendship of England.

Then followed the Russian war which obviously forms no part of my subject. It belongs to the history of Europe. Many of the events by which it was diversified, were highly honourable to the French arms, and no doubt can be entertained that the two nations acted together with energy and good faith. But it may be questioned whether the alliance has ever been cordial; in France, it has certainly not been regarded with a favourable eye; partly, perhaps, because it disappointed the hopes of the old military or Napoleonist faction, and partly because it thwarted the designs of the Legitimists, Orleanists, and Republicans.

It was, moreover, little agreeable to what may be called the real Catholic party, the intelligent members of which must have perceived from the beginning that Louis Napoleon regarded the Church exclusively as an instrument and its ministers as sacerdotal slaves.

All the traditions and associations of Catholicism in France are connected with the Bourbons, and if the Republicans were wise they would seek on this point to supplant their rivals, and connect themselves with religion, not merely out of reverence for the thing itself, but as the only means of political success.

While these transactions were in progress, Louis Napoleon married the Countess de Teba, a Spanish lady of respectable family. His declaration on this occasion was full of manly and independent sentiments. In selecting a wife, he said he had consulted less the necessities of his position than the affections of his heart. This language would have produced more effect on the mind of Europe, had the fact not been well known that he had previously made overtures for the daughters of several royal families, and been rejected. When princesses proved coy, it was found that the Countess de Teba would do· well enough for a fortunate parvenu.

Upon the attempt to assassinate him, upon his visit to England, and on the visit of the queen of this country to France, it is wholly unnecessary to enter into details, because they are events without any political significance. The only remaining subject worthy of attention is the conclusion of peace with Russia, in which Louis Napoleon has acted a prominent part. It is probable, however, that even the plenipotentiaries of the various Powers assembled in Paris, were not cognisant of all the facts which had led to that result. Louis Napoleon imitates, as far as practicable, the home policy of Russia, which considers the internal movements of society as things too domestic to be disclosed to foreigners.

We are not sufficiently acquainted with the state of France to be able to decide how far the condition of the people influenced the resolutions of the Government; whether the resources of the country showed signs of exhaustion, and whether, in consequence, the population gave tokens of dissatisfaction, which suggested to the rulers that it would be prudent to lay on the people no more burdens, but to put an end to the war with all practicable speed. It is said, upon grounds which appear to be by no means slight, that Bonapartism is on the wane in the provinces, where knowledge of some kind or another is diffusing itself, and giving rise to a strong desire for free institutions.

If this desire be not gratified, the fault may in some measure perhaps be attributed to the Republican party. After many years of disaster; after having been decimated again and again by despotism; after having thrown up barricades over nearly the whole surface of France ; after having shed the blood of brave and devoted men in torrents; after having been proscribed by every successive government from the eighteenth Brumaire until now, the members of that party have not yet learned wisdom.

France enjoyed a considerable amount of liberty under the restored dynasty, which, by judicious management, might have been gradually augmented, until the nation was satisfied with the recognition of its rights and privileges. Through the intrigues of the house of Orleans, a revolution was brought about, and a revolutionary monarchy established with a citizen king at its head. But, somehow, royal houses in France find it difficult to ally themselves with freedom. Louis Philippe was greedy of power, and the liberal party was intolerant of the slightest check. The consequence was the revolution of February, and the establishment of a Republic.

What then ? Were the French people contented ? No; having conquered the government of their choice, they wished to proceed further into the unknown regions of politics, to explore the hidden foundations of property, to organise labour upon principles not recognised by nature, and instead of resting satisfied with having established a new government, aimed at reconstructing the whole me-

chanism of social life. This alarmed the wealthy,
and made them ready to throw themselves into the
arms of any one who would undertake to deliver
them from the evils they dreaded.

No harm would have befallen them, had they remained true to the Republic. Their taxes were moderate, their duties were light, their security and
tranquillity complete. But wild people talked and
wrote wildly, in conformity with their nature; their
speculations were daring, their paradoxes terrific;
but practically they would have acted like other
people, and left the whole social edifice much as
they found it. But the opulent and the privileged
are always timid, and being ignorant besides, were
easily persuaded that there is no stability in freedom.
They never had been free, and being therefore completely without experience, and disliking the only
free communities they knew, — Great Britain and
Switzerland, - they fancied it would be better for
their interests to have a strong government. In
fact, they were afraid of the Republicans, who enjoyed and laughed at their fears, instead of wisely
seeking to calm or dissipate them.

Hence Louis Napoleon came to be looked upon
by capitalists, wealthy proprietors, dealers in stocks,
in railway shares, in merchandise of all kinds, as a

sort of social deliverer. The peasantry went like cattle in whatever way they were driven, and so the second Empire was established. Then, as might have been foreseen, the greatest possible disappointment followed. Instead of a diminution of taxes, there was an immense increase, partly to pay the army which had been augmented the better to keep down the people, partly to defray the expenses of rebuilding half Paris, partly to meet the enormous expenditure of the Russian war. Now, therefore, it is said, even the rural population begins to look back with envy at the brief but golden days of the Republic, when they were asked to pay very little; when fathers and sons were not taken from the plough to cut the throats of other fathers and sons in distant provinces; when every man might think as he pleased, and speak as he thought; when journals good, bad, and indifferent, supplied those who read with new amusement every hour; when there was a constant succession of harmless fêtes, planting and blessing trees of liberty, meetings in the open air, meetings in cafés; a kind of life, in short, not unlike what we enjoy here in these islands, except that there was a little more bustle, a little more gaiety, considerably more dancing, and a great deal less drunkenness.

The French now look back upon all these things

as the several families of the world look back upon
the Golden Age, that is to say, as a thing gone for
ever. What they have at present to do is to work
hard, to pay their taxes, buy images or engravings
of Louis Napoleon to show their loyalty, and never
to open their mouths on the subject of politics. If
you ask them a question which has the most distant
bearing on public affairs, they reply, " We know
nothing about it, it is not our business; d'ye see
there are *gendarmes* about; and then what would
you ? it is much better to be silent."

Louis Napoleon has an ear much larger and more
terrible than that of Dionysius. Everybody in
France knows this, and consequently everybody
fears.

The treaty of peace with Russia closed one particular period of Louis Napoleon's life, and opened
another. The English alliance has borne fruit, —
barren victories, and a war terminated from exhaustion. France is once more free to form new alli-
ances more in accordance with the principles by
which her government is regulated, and public
opinion already points to the North as the scene
on which Louis Napoleon's diplomacy is likely next
to develope itself. But a man may have more
tendencies than appear on the surface of his cha-

racter, and he may therefore determine to disappoint
by his prudence and moderation the anticipations of
mankind.

His position in France is beset with difficulties
I might perhaps say with dangers.   A large portion
of the nation, over which he holds sway, is inimical
to his rule; many sympathise with the Italians
with the Hungarians, with the Poles, with the
Greeks.   He has made himself responsible in some
measure for the behaviour of the Papal Government
by crushing the Roman Republic and restoring
the Pope's authority.   After several years of expe
rience, however, it now appears that no progress a
all has been made in Central Italy towards good
government.   The authorities dread the people
and the people detest the authorities.   Nothing bu
foreign bayonets now upholds the sacerdotal des
potism.   Withdraw the props, and down at once goes
the edifice.

Misgovernment is no less flagrant in the kingdom
of Naples, where thousands of enlightened and
liberal men, whose only crime is their attachment to
their country, lie rotting in prisons, in some case
far below the level of the sea, where reptiles, and
damp, and noisome effluvia continue to sap the force
of life.   Louis Napoleon stands pledged to endea
vour in conjunction with England to abate this evil.

At the same time, to illustrate the anomalies of his situation, I may allude to his hostility to the liberty of the press in Belgium. His plenipotentiary at the Conferences invited the representatives of the other Powers to consider that question, with a view to curtail the freedom which public opinion vindicates to itself in that country. Louis Napoleon is not unacquainted with English literature, and may remember with profit an observation of Lord Bacon. The only way, he says, "to destroy bad books, is to write good ones." Apply the remark to journals. If the Belgians encourage bad papers, let the journalists of Paris be let loose against them, and the genius of France, if Louis Napoleon can contrive to enlist it on his side, will soon make short work with the Brussels politicians.

But he is afraid, it may be said, of the press of his own country, and has therefore put it down. So much the worse for him, since this only proves that a majority of men in France who think and reason and write are against him. In other words, the intelligence of the country is inimical to his government. He therefore rules in opposition to the will of that portion of the people which understands what it is to have a will of its own, and has nothing on his side but that physical force

with which despotism everywhere keeps down opinion. Still, so long as that force supports him, he
will continue Emperor of the French.

According to the report of many observers, public
opinion in France is flowing rapidly away from the
Tuileries. People have not found themselves in
that millennium which Marshal St. Arnaud fancied
he saw begin in 1852. On the contrary, even the
Bonapartists themselves have been deceived in their
hopes; perhaps they looked for too much; perhaps
they were capricious; perhaps events have occurred
which have necessarily given a new direction to
their ideas. Even the English alliance, useful as
it has been in some sense to Louis Napoleon, may
in other respects have tended greatly to abridge his
popularity. Yet, having entered upon this policy,
it will be his wisest course to persevere in it, and
by enlarging the commercial intercourse between
the two nations to give to the industrious classes a
powerful material reason for attaching themselves to
his government.

Of course he has sufficient foresight to comprehend
that if he resolves upon adopting this policy he will
soon find himself under the necessity of opening and
enlarging the political institutions of France; for
free trade implies other kinds of freedom. An im-

mense commerce, carried on with energy and intelligence, presupposes in the people the existence of
mental qualities which are irreconcilable with slavery.
The interests of the trading classes can be properly
watched over only by their own representatives in
a parliament which has the power to make its decrees
respected. Establish such a parliament in France,
and Louis Napoleon must cease to be emperor, and
pass into a new category of royalty, less pompous,
but far more elevated.

If he discovers in time the wisdom of this course,
he may check a reaction which has already commenced, and which will either restore the old
legitimate line of princes or again lead to the proclamation of a Republic. In any case I fear that France
will not speedily see an end of her troubles. Her inhabitants are too enlightened for despotism without
being sufficiently enlightened for freedom. They are
therefore obviously in a transition state, and as the
great pendulum of public opinion oscillates, will
alternately retrograde and advance, until a knowledge
of politics shall be sufficiently diffused among the
people to render practicable the reign of liberty.

I do not pretend to foresee what part Louis Napoleon will choose to play in this prodigious drama ;
but, judging from his antecedents, I am not at all

inclined to argue that it will be a noble or honourable part. There is a taint in his blood; he springs from a bad stock; he has no sympathy with free institutions, no love for the people. All his leanings are dynastic, and by professing faith in destiny, he has provided himself beforehand with an excuse for any crimes he may commit. He will always think it sufficient to attribute them to the overruling influence of his star. Against such a man the citizens of a free country cannot be too much on their guard.

CHAP. XI.

ACTUAL POSITION OF LOUIS NAPOLEON.

If we now inquire what useful lesson is taught by the preceding narrative, the answer, it appears to me, is this: that no reliance is to be placed on the professions of Louis Napoleon. All men, it is commonly believed, make their own interest the centre of their ideas, plans, and actions, and the exceptions are perhaps too few to disturb the foundations of the general principle. Louis Napoleon, however, greatly transcends what is ordinary in the application of this law. During his childhood, his youth, and his early manhood, he seems to have been remarkable rather than otherwise for his generosity, and had he succeeded peacefully to a throne, might have always continued so. But forty years of his life were given up to vicissitude — to struggles — to uncertainty — to plots — to stratagems — to impostures   to disappointments.

All this period he probably looked upon as thrown away, and when circumstances placed before him the chance of making up for lost time he seized upon it with eagerness, and resolved to make use of all means, no matter how iniquitous, to enjoy the intoxicating sweets of ambition. Being a man of sagacity, he had been frank with himself if with no one else; and had made and acknowledged the discovery that no road to fame lay open to him, save that which he has since trodden.

While he possessed no other means of distinction he had tried literature, but tried it in vain. His books had no vitality in them; they gave evidence of considerable knowledge, of talent, industry, and observation; but the fire of genius was wanting. The author never being warm himself, necessarily failed to impart warmth to his readers. It was evident he had thought much, and passed under review the whole system of modern civilisation, the growth of states, the relations of empires, the probabilities and prospects of revolutions. But he had done all this from a peculiar point of view; that is, to ingratiate himself with the French people in order that he might become their master.

He had travelled through several countries and received much kindness from foreigners, but contracted no friendships, indulged in no confidences, believed in no professions, and never deserved that any faith should be placed in him. The opinions he

put forward were such as he thought best calculated
to promote his interest.   Together with his brother
Napoleon he was in early life a Republican, a conspirator, and an insurrectionist, denounced the Pope
as a tyrant, and the clergy as time-servers, and
sought actively to put an end to sacerdotal domina-
tion.

When he had occasion to speak of his uncle's rule,
he condemned it as arbitrary, and accounted for his
overthrow by the excess of his despotism.   Nothing
could satisfy his mind but the extreme of democracy.
He came to England, he associated with our privileged classes, and when to superficial observers it
seemed likely that a contest would arise between
the democracy and the government, he abandoned
the former, and, as far as he was permitted, took up
a position against them.   When power came to him,
he denounced all attempts at converting his democratic theories into practice as mere Utopias, and
spoke of his former friends as incorrigible persons,
who were labouring to raise a storm by which they
would be the first to perish.

The study of his letters, speeches, proclamations, manifestoes, while creating a highly favourable
opinion of his skill and abilities, must at the same
time convince us of the entire want of high

principle in his mind. He excels in short, terse, vigorous compositions, but appears to be soon exhausted, and to pause for want of materials. This is the reason why his books are inferior. He has no fixed principles or opinions, and his thoughts refuse to assume any settled form. When he is desirous of putting his hand upon them, they glide away like globules of quicksilver, enlarging, diminishing, agglomerating, separating, in obedience to some law which regulates irresistibly the creations of his mind.

But with all this fluctuation of means and instruments, he has with inflexible steadiness pursued the track of his own advancement. From this he has never swerved, even for an instant. To gratify the cravings of his ambition, he has considered no means unlawful—fraud, deception, perjury, oppression, exile, massacre. Nor when he had obtained his point did he shrink from acknowledging his crimes. He described them, it is true, by periphrases, by skilful, extenuating language, by sophisms, by fallacies; but conscious he had been acting in the sight of all Europe he felt it would be absurd to affect disguise, and he has accordingly affected none.

If this be a true picture of the man, it must

obviously be impossible to reckon very confidently
on the stability of an alliance with him. His
political principles are the antipodes of ours. Looking at the condition of Europe, he may for some
time discover reasons for preferring the friendship
of England to that of any other state ; but if the
history of modern times teach any particular lesson,
it is, I think, this, that no continental power, and
least of all France, has any very cordial attachment
for England.

It could serve no useful purpose to disguise
the fact, that we are a nation apart, that our institutions, our laws, our manners, our religion,
in short, everything in our civil polity and social
life tends to make us different from our neighbours. The very fact of our being a free people
renders us obnoxious to nearly the whole continent. We are considered and spoken of abroad as
the originators and apostles of revolution, because
they cannot distinguish between the quiet enjoyment of freedom and the desire to subvert and
destroy. But as far as we have any political
sympathies, they must obviously be extended to
those governments which most resemble our own.
No doubt when we have formed an alliance even
with despotisms, we shall be careful honourably to

fulfil all the conditions which such a state of things imposes on us. But in case of any great struggle on the Continent, our leanings would inevitably be towards the partisans of free institutions.

It may consequently happen, that the complications which cannot fail to arise in the affairs of Europe, will compel us to adopt a policy different from that of Louis Napoleon. As long as the alliance can be maintained with advantage to the two countries, I trust it will be preserved inviolate : but it seems probable that Louis Napoleon, clear-seeing as he is, may yet, when troubles again arise in Christendom, fail to understand his best interests, and through the influence of his feelings be tempted to form new political combinations. Several powerful governments are at this moment intriguing for the support of France, and it is difficult to foresee in what direction her views of her own interest will precipitate her. If, in conjunction with England, she should attempt the reconstruction of the Italian States, a rupture with the court of Vienna would be the almost necessary consequence. On the other hand, considerations arising out of the state of Eastern Europe may render a proper understanding with Russia impracticable.

In whatever light viewed, the alliance of England

with Louis Napoleon is surrounded by uncertainty.
He may soon have to wage a civil war with his own
countrymen. The elements of disaffection, which
have never ceased to exist, though enveloped for
awhile with obscurity, are diffusing themselves, and
acquiring fresh force every day. The working
classes, for whom he has invariably expressed so
much sympathy, have throughout the greater part
of France witnessed the complete blighting of their
hopes. A large portion of the country lies unculti-
vated, because very little is done towards rendering
rural industry profitable. Peace will throw large
masses of men out of employment, and send them
back into the provinces to augment the difficulties of
the country.

Commerce meanwhile languishes, and the new
combinations which threaten to take place in the
political world may tend still further to disorganise
the resources of France. To accelerate this result,
the ignorance and obstinacy of the people frustrate
the endeavours of the government to introduce free
trade. On this subject Louis Napoleon is far in
advance of the French nation. He seeks to remove
the shackles from industry, the mass of the people
resist; he offers them an immense boon, but they
refuse it; and at the least approach to an enlightened

political economy assemble tumultuously together, and conjure the government to preserve their commercial chains.

The new-born peace, whether short-lived or not, can hardly be expected to prove anything but a respite to the troubles of France. The government is widely unpopular; immense masses of ignorance on the one hand and a large amount of intelligence on the other are arrayed against it, and it is impossible to foresee to what extent Louis Napoleon will be able to resist the pressure which may be brought to bear upon his government. The rivalry of the two nations sleeps, but is not extinguished. An entirely free government in France might have gone far towards obliterating it; but a military despotism, however disguised, is little calculated to produce this desirable result. Commerce, industry, intelligence, a free. press, and complete personal liberty might have drawn closer the links of friendship with England.

But the supporters of Louis Napoleon's government are the military classes, and it is among these almost exclusively that hatred of England exists. In proportion, therefore, as his situation is dominated by the army will be the difficulty of preserving the present alliance. Diplomacy can achieve

very little towards bringing two nations long hostile
into a cordial disposition towards each other. This
must be done by the diffusion of sound ideas and
manly and honourable sentiments, and Louis Napoleon has annihilated the only instrument by
which it is possible to carry on this process. The
French provinces are compelled to grovel in the
thickest darkness, and must depend for all their
ideas of us and our government upon the distorted
traditions of the empire, which are all hostile to us.

If Louis Napoleon desires to be the real friend
of England, he must commence by becoming the
liberator, not the enslaver of France, whose inhabitants have at length been surfeited with military
glory, and are desirous of grasping something more
tangible. In fact, they would prefer a little liberty
—real, moderate, constitutional liberty, which allies
itself naturally with industry, with the arts of peace,
with the progress of civilisation.

It would sometimes almost appear as if he himself
likewise took this view. Towards the close of 1856,
the hostility of several imperial *préfets* and municipal
institutions received a check from the Minister of the
Interior, who was commanded by the emperor to
inform them that in all matters not bearing directly
upon state affairs the people were to be allowed to

manage their own concerns. But from this solitary example it would be unsafe to draw any very cheering inference. Still everything is deserving of notice which serves to indicate the inclination of the French government to improve its domestic policy; and if Louis Napoleon comprehends this first necessity of France, and yields gracefully and in time to the wishes of the nation, he may continue to reign over one of the finest countries in Europe: if not, the fate of Napoleon, of Charles X., and Louis Philippe will be his.

THE END.

LONDON:
Printed by SPOTTISWOODE & Co.,
New-street-Square.

LIST OF AUTHORITIES

Mémoires de Tous. Collection de Souvenirs contemporains, tendant à établir la Vérité dans l'Histoire. 8vo. 6 vols.

Idées Napoléoniennes, par le Prince Napoléon Louis Bonaparte. 8vo.

Mémoires Anecdotiques sur l'Intérieur du Palais, et sur quelques Évènemens de l'Empire depuis 1805—1814. Par de Bausset. 8vo. 2 vols.

Mémoires sur Napoléon, le Directoire, le Consulat, l'Empire, et la Restauration. Par Bourrienne. 8vo. 10 vols.

Mémoires sur l'Impératrice Joséphine, ses Contemporains, la Cour de Navarre et de la Malmaison. Post 8vo. 2 vols.

Mémoires de Lucien Bonaparte, Prince de Canino. 8vo.

Mémoires historiques et secrètes de l'Impératrice Joséphine. Par Mme. le Normand. 8vo. 2 vols.

Mémoires sur Mme la Duchesse de St. Leu, ex-Reine de Hollande. 2 vols 8vo.

Mémoires sur la Reine Hortense et la Famille Impériale, par Mlle. Cochelet, Lectrice de la Reine (Mme. Parquin). 4 vols.

Mémoires sur la Cour de Louis Napoléon et sur la Hollande. 8vo.

Napoleon the Little. By Victor Hugo. Post 8vo.

Histoire des Crimes du deux Décembre. Par V. Schœlcher, Representant du Peuple. Post 8vo.

Le Coup d'État de Louis Bonaparte, Histoire de la Persécution de Décembre, Évènemens, Prisons, Casemates et Pontons. Par Xavier Durrien, ancien Représentant du Peuple. 8vo.

B B

Les Bonapartes depuis 1815 jusqu'à ce jour.   Par Félix Wonters.
Post 8vo.

Histoire de la Restauration,   Par Alphonse de Lamartine. 6 vols.
vo.

Lettres et Correspondance de St.-Arnaud.   2 vols. 8vo.

Portraits Politiques.   Vie de Louis Napoléou. Par La Guéronnière.
Post 8vo.

Secret Correspondence of the Emperor Nicholas with the British
Government.   Published by order of Parliament.   Folio.

Le Traité de Paix.   Par un ancien Diplomate.   8vo.

Œuvres de Napoléon III.   4 vols. 8vo.

Purple Tints of Paris.   By Bayle St. John.   2 vols. post 8vo.

Subalpine Kingdom.   By Bayle St. John.   2 vols. 8vo.

Histoire de Dix Ans, 1830—1840.   Par Louis Blanc.   5 vols.
8vo.

Organisation du Travail.   Par Louis Blanc.   Post 8vo.

Appel aux honnêtes Gens.   Par Louis Blanc.   Post 8vo.

Le Peuple, et la Voix du Peuple.   Par Proudhon.   2 vols. folio.

Projet de Constitution de la République Française.   Par Lamennais.   18mo.

Du Travail.   Par Lamennais.   18mo.

De la Famille.   Par Lamennais.   18mo.

Histoire du Consulat et de l'Empire.   Par Thiers.   10 vols. 8vo.

Le Consulat et l'Empire, ou Histoire de la France, et de Napoléon
Bonaparte, de 1799 à 1815.   Par Thibaudeau.   10 vols. 8vo.

Histoire de la France sous Louis Philippe. Par Capefigue. 8 vols.
8vo.

Les Diplomates Européens.   Par Capefigue.   2 vols. 8vo.

BIBLIOLIFE

1820268R0023

Printed in Great Britain
by Amazon.co.uk, Ltd.,
Marston Gate.